Th(Grounds!

Here, where we make our
greatest choice.

Rita and Owen Blake

Table of Contents

Acknowledgements

First of all we'd like to thank and acknowledge the Holy Spirit who told me to write this book even though I have never written one before. He said it will be unique and not to worry about my abilities and that He would use it for His purposes. We would also like to acknowledge our parents. We thank you for all the love you showered upon us, even when at times we were so unlovable. Our parents and parents in general, can be an example of Christ's love. Much love and appreciation to Shirley S., Ron D., Pat H. and Karen O. for all the help they gave us. You all are very wise and your hearts are filled with Jesus' love which brings joy to all those who have the privilege of your friendship.

Thank You!

Introduction

During the darkest, saddest time of my life, Satan was telling me to drive my car off a high bridge and end my misery. I might have done it except that the Holy Spirit was communicating with me as well through thought impressions and what the Bible refers to in 1ˢᵗ Kings 19 as the "still small voice," also known as a gentle whisper.

He was helping me to understand that there was an age-old battle going on in my mind, which is referred to as "the battle of truth verses lies." He made it clear that I was being attacked by Satan, God's enemy and our enemy.

Not all of the thoughts we have are our own. We must be aware that we have an enemy in the spiritual realm whose mission is to kill, steal and destroy. If he can kill you through suicide or use you to kill another through anger or selfishness, Satan has then accomplished his mission. If Satan can win you over and cause his evil to reign in your mind, body and soul then he has succeeded.

If Satan, the flesh or the world have caused evil and sin in your life and you have done something that seems unforgiveable, know that there is forgiveness in Jesus through His death on the cross. The enemy may win a battle or two but he will not win the war. This is true only if you come to Jesus. The power of the Holy Spirit and God's word, the Bible, will help you to identify the enemy you face and live a life pleasing to God.

The purpose of this book is to share with you the heartbreak, healing and restoration that we've experienced in life through a relationship with our Heavenly Father, through Jesus Christ and the Holy Spirit. It is our hope that through this book you'll have a better understanding of the works and purpose of the

Holy Spirit. Each chapter in this book represents a time when we needed God desperately and how He communicated with my husband and myself.

Background

I grew up with an alcoholic dad. Mom tried to hold it all together through prayers and lots of tears. My sister and three brothers were wonderful. I never lacked for love; however, fear and uncertainty in a home dominated by an alcoholic father was the norm for me. Mom and Dad both proclaimed to love Jesus. Mom tried to live it but Dad did not. He was disturbed mentally. He'd sit in his room and talk to people who weren't there. After I became a Christian I suspected he was communicating with demons. His conversations were bazaar and we chalked it up as part of the drunken behavior of an alcoholic.

Mom and Dad fought constantly and seemed to genuinely hate one another. At first Mom would tell Dad, "You're going to get cirrhosis of the liver if you don't stop drinking." As years went by her proclamation changed to, "I hope you get cirrhosis of the liver and die!" Dad would respond with, "I hope you die of cancer."

An interesting thing happened. Mom died of cirrhosis and Dad of cancer. Although Mom never drank, it was an adverse reaction to a diabetic medication that destroyed her liver. Dad died of cancer of the esophagus. The curses of sicknesses they wished on each other had come upon themselves. Mom would continually tell me how disgusted she was with my Dad. She didn't need to tell me anything because his behavior was enough to enlighten me as to how despicable he was … I hated him. The hate for my Dad was constant because of his behavior and Mom's hate for him was like a volcano that would erupt onto anyone near her. A good part of Mom's conversation consisted of how much she despised him.

I was twelve years old when they separated. It was the most peaceful three months of my existence. At the end of that three months Mom said, "Come sit down children, I have good news for you. Your Dad's coming home!" I was so sad and distraught in my heart. I think that was the first time I understood the meaning of "depression." I wondered why she would choose to let that mean man back into our lives.

When I was around thirteen or fourteen I ran away from home for a few months and began my own messy journey. I ended up on the streets of New Mexico with my girlfriend. We stopped by the Salvation Army kitchen for a bite to eat and ended up hearing a message about God's forgiveness. I accepted the Lord Jesus Christ as my personal Savior that day. I was compelled by the Holy Spirit to call home immediately, which I did.

I was so happy to talk with my mom and she urged me to come home at once. I felt like the prodigal son the Bible refers to in Luke 15:11-32. Most parents have a love for their children that is similar to that which God has for us, even when we are making a mess out of our lives. I had put Mom through despair because she didn't know if I was dead or alive. My oldest brother comforted Mom through those tough times of anguish. She was falling apart and he had to be the adult, holding it all together for her. My brother was only fifteen at the time. The emotional turmoil he had to endure was tremendous. Dad wasn't able to support Mom emotionally, and of course, he cared less about what was happening to me; he continued on his alcoholic path.

I was very fortunate to have a mom who gave me unconditional love. Mom was an excellent example of the love of God in my life.

Many years later after Dad died, Mom had a death bed experience. Jesus told her, "Diane get right with your husband!" God was telling Mom to forgive Dad. God doesn't want us holding on to anger, grudges or hatred against anyone. It's important for our own sake that we are to forgive those who have wronged us. God tells us that we are to forgive others because He has forgiven us for so much in salvation.

I learned that I needed to go to my Heavenly Father and ask His forgiveness, then do my best to turn from my destructive lifestyle. He would give me the power to be successful. The Holy Spirit longs to communicate with us and to make us holy. Leonard Ravenhill put it like this:

> *"The greatest miracle that God can do today is to take an unholy man out of an unholy world, and make that man holy and put him back into that unholy world and keep him holy in it."* [1]

I was sincere in the salvation prayer that I prayed that day at the Salvation Army. Although I came home not knowing the importance of reading my Bible and attending church, I continued to make one mistake after another with God pulling me out of sin and evil as best He could. Because God gives us a free will, He will not interfere with my bad choices and I will in one way or another experience the consequences from my actions.

I graduated from high school and entered college. After about a year and a half of college I met my first husband, Damion, and we were married. I did not meet him in college but through a friend who told me, "Damion is no good. Stay away from him." After multiple beatings I realized my friend was

---

[1] http://www.ravenhill.org/heartb12.htm. "Excerpts from 'Heart Breathings.'"

right. He was not good and I should have stayed away from him. Damion had been in and out of trouble with the law and had recently been released from prison when I met him. He had a hard heart and I was too gullible to know what that would ultimately bring. I was naive in many regards, always thinking people would be decent and fair.

Although my Dad was abusive to Mom, he was not as physically abusive as my first husband. Dad would hit Mom but he didn't punch her in the face, kick her nonstop while she was on the ground until it appeared she was dead like Damion did to me. I could not tell anyone what was going on because I did not want my brothers hurt by this maniac that I had carelessly married. It was not their problem, I thought. Because in some way, I had seen my mom abused by my dad throughout my life, abuse seemed normal.

At that point in my life there was not a day that did not include weeping and crying which continued for the years that I was married to Damion. That time was not long in comparison to some marriages, but when you're being beaten daily, and crying is a normal part of your lifestyle, any amount of time can seem like an eternity.

Damion and I were ready for a change. We wanted to change our life in a positive way. He decided to join the Army. Off he went hoping that life was going to be better for us with him in the military. His brother was in the military doing quite well for himself and he thought that this was the way out for us. After four months, Damion was thrown out of the Army due to his past imprisonment. He convinced me to join, which I did. Our marriage ended in divorce several years later.

While I was in the Army I was experimenting in the occult by reading tarot cards, fortune telling and having séances. I didn't think there was any harm in séances. I thought of them as fun and entertaining. It was something that was becoming a part of my life and I didn't think of it in terms of being evil. Just because I didn't think of something as evil does not necessarily mean it is not evil.

As things progressed down this occult playground, furniture would start moving and spiritual apparitions became apparent; they would continue after the séance was over. It was quite spooky. I thought I was losing my mind. Eventually, I discovered that nothing stopped this but the Name of "Jesus."

While I was involved in the occult, my sister Maria, who was a born-again Christian, shared the gospel with me. I knew that Jesus' name was the only power I had in fighting the evil that was being manifested and brought on by my dark behavior. Maria explained that I needed Jesus because we are all sinners. We think we are good and deserve whatever we want, but next to our holy God, we are like filthy rags and need Jesus' cleansing to have a right standing with Him.

Nothing else can cleanse us but Jesus' blood that was shed on the cross. Only by true faith in Jesus and a humble repentance, turning from our sinful ways, can we make Jesus our Lord and Master. He gives us a right standing with our Father God who is in Heaven and will not judge us for our sins. By doing this we can have eternal life and can enter Heaven when we die. That is the Gospel; the very good news that Maria shared with me.

I was trying desperately to satisfy a need for something but I was looking in the wrong places. I didn't know about demonic spirits that could communicate with me and possibly lead me into wickedness, evil and all forms of darkness. I was trying to satisfy the spiritual side of myself with the occult, not knowing that Jesus was the answer and that Jesus was willing to give me His precious Holy Spirit to fill that void in my heart. Although I had accepted Jesus Christ as my Savior when I was fourteen, those wrong choices, neglecting the importance of reading the Bible, not going to church and not associating with Christians hindered the Holy Spirit's work in my life. I knew that I needed to rededicate myself to the Lord as I had not been making good choices pleasing to God.

At twenty-three when my contract with the Army was over I went back to live with my parents. One Sunday around 3:00 in the afternoon my sister Maria asked if I wanted to go to church with her. We agreed to go to church and dinner afterwards. The church she took me to was named "Happy Church." The Pastor gave a great sermon and it spoke volumes to me. Toward the end of the sermon he asked, "Is there anyone in the room who wants to accept Jesus Christ as Lord and Savior? Raise your hand if this is you."

My hand went up fast. Then he said, "If you raised your hand come forward for prayer." I was extremely shy at that time, so when I jumped up and ran to where the Pastor was standing I surprised myself. The Pastor had all the people in the church, about a thousand people, point their hands toward me as they prayed.

Even now the remembrance of those precious people and their out stretched hands and prayers warms my heart. I was now definitely feeling the indwelling of the Holy Spirit. I needed this rededication to God and surrendering to Jesus this second time. Now I was more of an adult and was guided to do what a mature Christian should do. I read my Bible daily, attended church, prayed and grew in obedience to what God was calling me to become. I had finally learned how to allow the Holy Spirit to do what He does best; make me Holy, bit by bit.

The first thing that hit me when I left church that morning, to my surprise, was how much I now loved my dad. Dad had not changed anything to bring about this love. Jesus changed my heart that night when I went forward. Instead of being a person that had a heart full of hate, I now had a heart full of love. The greatest manifestation of that love was displayed in the love I have had for my Dad from that moment forward. It's pure, clean and unconditional love. The kind of love God has for us. What a great feeling it was to love my crusty old, alcoholic Dad. To be released of all those years of hatred toward him was a miracle! He had not changed, but I could now see him through the eyes of love and compassion.

When God opens our eyes to see through His eyes we see truth with clarity. This man, my dad, was making unwise decisions based on his own sin filled, selfish choices, and life experiences which were not in harmony with God's will. The people around him suffered because they were the recipients of the consequences of his bad choices. These types of sinful, selfish, prideful people are to be pitied, prayed for and if at all possible, brought to an understanding of their sinfulness in light of God's perfect holiness. We must be humbled before God by acknowledging our life of sin. We are all broken toys in need of repair, some more so than others. In a way my dad was a teacher, teaching me what not to do and who I did not want to become.

God took my old, dirty, ugly heart that day at the Happy Church and gave me a sparkling clean, soft, tender heart full of love. What a joy to be able to love the unlovable. God loved me even when I was so unlovable. After my salvation and from that time on, the grass always looked greener and the rocks and mountains more beautiful, the sky is ever so blue. My life became more real and truly purposeful. I was set free. Set free to love rather than harshly judge and hate. Wow!

My Dad knew there was a change in me as the dynamics of our relationship changed. He knew I loved him and now I knew he always had loved me and his other four children to the best of his ability. He has since gone home to be in heaven and I was blessed to be with him on his last day and prayed with him. I know he's whole in heaven now and not the man he used to be here on earth, but he is now the man God had always intended him to be. I'm happy for him.

My sister thinks Mom and Dad never cross paths in heaven or it would not be heaven. She must think they still hate each other but I think they are the best of friends. We could not possibly be residents in heaven and have a heart of hate or it would not be heaven. Forgiveness is a big part of a healthy spiritual life.

Helpful Ideas

♥ **Ephesians 4: 31 & 32 (NLT)**
"Get rid of all bitterness, rage, anger, harsh words, and slander, as well as all types of evil behavior. Instead, be kind to each other, tender hearted, forgiving one another, just as God through Christ has forgiven you."

♥ **Ephesians 5: 17 & 18 (NLT)**
"Don't act thoughtlessly, but understand what the Lord wants you to do. Don't be drunk with wine, because that will ruin your life. Instead, be filled with the Holy Spirit."

How to Forgive

- ♥ One important way to destroy any anger towards someone is to pray for them, the more you pray, the more anger will subside and forgiveness will become easier.

- ♥ Memorizing a forgiveness scripture is an excellent thing to do.

- ♥ Consider memorizing Ephesians 4:31-32 (above).

- ♥ Remember, to forgive doesn't always mean to forget. You must be wise and be on guard; in other words, respect is earned but forgiveness is free.

- ♥ Forgiveness frees you from bitterness. Bitterness brings you harm.

- ♥ Unforgiveness hurts YOU. It is wise to forgive because it brings blessings.

- ♥ If someone you know refuses to change their bad behavior towards you or others, do not think that you need to make yourself available to that person. What you do need to do is to forgive. Pray for them and leave them in God's very capable hands.

- ♥ Forgiveness is an act based on faith. You're forgiving because God has forgiven you. Don't trust your feelings. Forgive by faith and eventually your feelings will likely follow; but even if they don't, continue trusting God. It's His will for you to forgive and He will reward you for your obedience.

- ♥ The Holy Spirit is God living in us; He is nurturing, comforting and guiding. Nevertheless, He is expectant and desires us to be obedient. Especially in forgiveness.

Experiencing the Holy Spirit

The first time I felt the presence of the Holy Spirit I was in church at the age of seven. Mom was determined that her children were to have the advantages that she thought they would need to be happy and successful in life. To her, that meant sending her children to the best school possible. She volunteered in the cafeteria at St. Joseph's Catholic School so that she could get a discount on the tuition and make it affordable for her children to attend. The beautiful thing about the Catholic school was that the awareness of God was part of our daily life through prayer, Bible studies and attending church. Although I'm no longer Catholic, I will never regret going to that school.

One wintery day in Colorado, as snowflakes fell ever so softly on our bundled up bodies, my class was walking from church back to the school, which was down the block and across the street. We were bathed in the Love of the Lord. That morning in the church toward the end of the service, we sang a song known to most Christians called "Holy, Holy, Holy." The Holy Spirit came down and enveloped the sanctuary with peace, love and joy. It was as if we somehow knew we were in the presence of God.

After singing that song, church was dismissed and we walked back to school, subdued, serene and peaceful. We were the quietest little seven-year-olds on the planet at that moment. It was so heavenly that I remember it to this day; the love of God that surrounded our precious little hearts. The times we are aware of God's presence are remarkably pure and unmistakably holy.

Helpful Ideas

Becoming aware of the Holy Spirit

- ♥ Titus **3: 6 (GNB)**
  God poured out the Holy Spirit abundantly on us through Jesus Christ our Savior.

- ♥ Memorize Romans 8: 6 (NASB)
  For the mind set on the flesh is death, but the mind set on the Spirit is life and peace.

- ♥ Come to God with child-like faith and trust. Please don't be confused; I'm not talking about immature childish behavior but like a child with pure, untainted and trusting faith.

- ♥ Sing to God. It may be an old Christmas song or hymn you learned as a child or any song that speaks of God's love. Sing it to God. My sister Maria was about three or four years old and had memorized a song playing on the radio, "I'm Henry the Eighth, I Am," made popular by Herman's Hermits in 1964. My parents would have her sing that song to any and every one that came to visit. It was a treat for all. If my parents loved hearing their child sing imagine how much more God would appreciate and enjoy hearing you singing to Him. It's true. The Bible says that God inhabits the praises of His people.

- ♥ **Psalm 96:1-2 (NIV)**
  Sing to the Lord a new song. Sing to the Lord, all the earth.

Suicide

I was caught up in some terrible lies during a certain time in my life. Satan planted thoughts of suicide in my mind. It was a sad time.

Walter, my second husband of 25 years, was diagnosed with lung cancer. Being Christians, we started to pray for his healing and went to the Pastor to have him lay hands on Walter for healing. There were other Christians praying for his recovery too. He had testicular cancer ten years prior to this diagnosis and had that part of his body amputated. At his ten year checkup we expected that he would be cancer free, we were surprised that lung cancer was discovered.

One night as I was working the swing shift, I took my break and I walked around the huge facility enjoying a few minutes of peace away from the stress associated with a 911 dispatch center. Not that every minute is a panic, it's just that you don't know when it's coming so the anticipation is high and taking these breaks are a time of sweet calming peace.

During this break the Holy Spirit told me in that still small voice, "Your husband is not going to recover. The prayers for his healing will not be answered. There's no need to panic, you still have quite a bit of time together." This information was a relief for me for some reason. When God speaks to us and allows us to know His will, it's a time of acceptance, understanding and love all bound up together. It makes one content knowing that our Father knows all things and works all things together for good, despite the fact that the outcome may not be what we would pick if it were left up to us.

We spent the next year and a half saying goodbye, wrapped up in chemo therapy and radiation. We were well prepared for his step into eternity when the doctor asked me to sign documents releasing him from life support. Several people were in the room with me for his final departure, his brother and sister-in-law, our Pastor and his wife, and Walter's cousin. He was unconscious, with tubes in his mouth and nose. His body was no longer working and the doctor explained the fluid coming from the tubes was drainage from his kidneys, which were shutting down.

It was such a sterile environment, very clean and modern. It seemed like there was no warmth or life permeating from that place. After I signed the papers to have life support removed, we were standing around Walter's bed, hushed and subdued. Someone came and removed the tubes from Walter's body. After a few minutes he began his final breathing, which was like gurgles of air that were escaping from his body as the breath of life left him. He then suddenly opened his eyes and became aware of his surroundings. There was joy and happiness radiating from his face and he seemed to be looking at a being, someone who was located on his right towards the ceiling. His facial expressions were saying, "I'm ready. May I go with you?" Then his body died and his spirit left.

Walter's mother had been living with us for the past twenty plus years and this was her first child to die. Even though Walter was sixty-four years old, to a mother a child is a child no matter the age. We mourned for about six months. One day she handed me an envelope full of marriage and divorce certificates that belonged to my deceased husband. These papers were a part of his life I knew nothing about. I was surprised and became quite suspicious which prompted me to look at his emails.

His emails indicated there had been adulteries. I started questioning his friends about his secret life and they confirmed my suspicions. I was devastated. Now I was no longer mourning his death but the death of the perfect marriage that I thought we had. My tears dried up much like a loaf of bread left baking for days, light as a feather and burnt to a crisp.

At the same time my work was becoming extremely stressful. Not so much due to the work, but to the constant harassment from management. We had gone from 911 dispatching for one city to dispatching for the entire west coast. With this change came new management, new software and plenty of new expectations. Most of the older workers were compelled to quit and I was no exception. Added to all of this, I was entering the age of menopause.

The combination of Walters's adultery, my job and menopause made me vulnerable to Satan's onslaught of his wickedness. While driving over a high bridge on my way home from work this thought came to me, "Drive off the bridge and end it all." The same thoughts came to me for several weeks every time I drove over that bridge. The Holy Spirit revealed to me that these thoughts were not my thoughts. Satan was trying to get me to kill myself.

Each time in the following days that I drove over that bridge it would become a serious time of prayer. During these prayer times God revealed some of the sins in my life. I was mad at God for sending me a husband that was such a cheat and disappointment. God told me that He had tried to let me know about his un-Christ-like behavior, but I did not hear because I had made Walter my idol. That's a sin. It's one of the Ten Commandments: *"Thou shall have no other gods before me."*

Walter always called me Pollyanna and I wondered, "Why?" One day I asked him and he said it was "because you my dear always wanted to believe the best of everything." We had a very happy marriage, at least I did. In my foolishness I was not able to distinguish fantasy from reality. I do believe that Walter was sexually addicted. I think he was into the immature thrill of falling in love with someone new every now and then. When he got tired of them he'd come back to me and I'd be someone new for a while.

I had evidence of his cheating, such as emails, letters, documents and a few of his friends telling me what took place, all to support the truth of his sexual addiction. Sometime later the Lord shared with me that Walter was not capable of being a devoted husband because he did not love Jesus enough.

During our marriage my devotion to God was sincere and reverent. I had no idea I was idolizing this man. God never gives us more than we can handle and I think the Lord allowed me to come to the truth when it was the best timing for me, about six months after Walter's death. I was a Pollyanna to the very last day of his life on earth. In many ways it was fortunate for both of us. If I had found out about his cheating while he was still alive I would have wanted to destroy him.

I used to wonder why Walter would listen to Dr. Laura over and over. Her tactic was; never tell your spouse that you had an affair if you want to stay married to that person. Don't confess; bear the burden on your own shoulders. I think she was his voice of reason even though misguided.

After discovering his adulteries I decided to stop mourning and move on with life. I joined a line dancing class thinking I would find Mr. Right dancing his little heart out in the class. Not! That class was full of women. I decided to stay for the exercise because it was a lot of fun. One day prior to going into class, I was in the parking lot leaning up against my van asking God, "Why couldn't you give me a husband who loved me only?" I was crying and trying to get myself together so that I could go into class. The Holy Spirit told me, "Can't you just forgive?" I said, "NO."

God understands everything about us and loves us anyway. He was working on my heart even when I was so wrapped up in hate and un-forgiveness. Forgiveness is a major part of healing. In First John 1:9, the Bible says, *"If we confess our sins He is faithful and just to forgive us our sins, and to cleanse us from all unrighteousness."* I did finally confess my sin of un-forgiveness towards Walter and I trusted God with His love and mercy to help me in forgiving Walter. God was moving me toward true forgiveness. It was a slow, tedious process. My hurt was deep and crushing and God loved me through it.

Walter was a professional drummer. Most of his affairs were with singers from the bands he performed with throughout the years of our marriage. I could not listen to any female singer without getting agitated after learning of his romances with female singers. Once I totally forgave Walter I was able to enjoy all music again. That was a happy day, but it took years to get there. Some healings are instantaneous and some healings take time. The wonderful news is that throughout the healing process God never leaves us or forsakes us.

Helpful Ideas

♥ When life's circumstances are unbearable and you're feeling desperate, call out to God. Read the Bible and trust God to pull you through and out of the darkness.

♥ **Proverbs 3:5-6 says,**
"Trust in the Lord with all your heart and lean not on your own understanding; in all your ways acknowledge Him, and He will make your paths straight." (Berean Study Bible)

♥ Do not trust in those self-destructive wicked thoughts; instead pull out a Bible and read, especially the New Testament. The Bible is God's Love Letter to you. Talk to God and listen for His answer. He quietly talks to me all the time and He is no respecter of persons. If He talks to me He wants to talk to you too. Expect to hear from Him in your heart and mind. We cannot have a real relationship without communication.

♥ Another thing you can do is ask for prayer. I remember once when I was at Costco to get a piece of pizza and I was terribly depressed. The Holy Spirit impressed upon me to go and ask this lady to pray for me. I went up to her and I asked, "Are you a Christian?" With a surprised look on her face she said, "Yes, I am." I then asked her if she would pray for me and she did. That prayer released me from a demonic thought process that had been bothering me for weeks. We who are children of God need each other, and praying for one another is a privilege. A true Christian will be so happy to pray for you, so please do not hesitate to ask for prayer.

♥ **Meditate on Jeremiah 29:11 (NIV)**
"For I know the plans I have for you," declares the Lord, "plans to prosper you and not to harm you, plans to give you hope and a future."

♥ **Read Romans 15:13 (NIV)**
"May the God of hope fill you with all joy and peace as you trust in him, so that you may overflow with hope by the power of the Holy Spirit."

♥ When you're being attacked by destructive thoughts especially that of suicide, remember that not all thoughts you have are your own thoughts. Sometimes Satan will come and whisper in your ear terrible lies. You can fight back by saying out loud a memorized Scripture, even if it's the same Scripture repeated over and over. Pray and ask the Holy Spirit to help you and to protect your mind. Whisper or shout a prayer. God's not hard of hearing. He'll hear the tiniest whisper to the loudest shout. Ask for His help wherever you are and in any circumstance. Let God guide you. Ask Him, "Who should I approach to ask for prayer?" Maybe God will send you to a church for prayer. In any event, get others to start praying for you. If you don't want to go to church call some of the churches and ask over the phone if they would pray for you.

♥ It's our privilege to pray for one another, so don't be shy to ask for prayer. Understand that you are not alone. Others are being attacked and are fighting the same battles. God is for you.

Murder

I was laying on the bed whimpering and crying with the smell of Iodoform disinfectant in the air adding to the foreign environment of the hospital. What should have been a safe place with quiet tranquility was anything but ... what I had just done removed any possibility of tranquility that could have been mine, not only for the moment but for years to come.

The nurses were floating around like quiet angels, nonjudgmental and serene. A man walked up to my bed and asked me, "What's wrong? Why are you crying?" This man was about 45, thin and Hispanic. His eyes were kind and caring. I told him what I had just done. I had just aborted a 17-week baby boy that fell into the toilet when it came out of me. The orderly then took it out of the toilet and threw it in a trash can like a soiled rag. I had just killed my baby. It's painful to know that I did that to an innocent child, I explained to him with tears rolling down my cheeks.

Abortion is such a monstrous act and terrorizing to an unborn baby. The man asked if we could pray. I agreed. He led me in a prayer where I asked God to forgive me for murdering this baby that ultimately belonged to God. For God is the giver of life. The unknown man left and I felt a peace and a calm come over me. Even so I would forever mourn this shameful act and the absolute selfishness of taking another's life.

It was particularly grievous because I had gone to the doctor for fertility pills to get pregnant in the first place. I was twenty-four at the time and had never been pregnant and desperately wanted a child. I didn't stop to consider that the man I was living with was not my husband and had no intention of becoming my husband. When I became pregnant it was unknown to me who the father really was. I was totally selfish when I chose to have the abortion. Nothing mattered to me but my convenience and wellbeing; otherwise I would have considered adoption. I did not want to raise a child alone and I didn't know what I would tell my child if he asked who his dad was. What a mess my promiscuity had created.

To add to the sin of murder I was also guilty of idolatry. I was idolizing myself. The idolatry of putting myself before God. I had made what I thought would be an inconvenience more important than the life of that innocent baby. Abortion was the ultimate act of the "Me Monster." Idolatry is one of the Ten Commandments in Exodus chapter 20. **"You shall have no other gods before Me."** **"You shall not murder"** is also one of the big ten. I could have put the baby up for adoption.

I had put my needs over the will of God. My will was more important than following God's good plan for the baby and me. So sinfully sad.

Owen, my current husband, was in his late twenties when he encouraged his pregnant girlfriend to have an abortion. They had been dating off and on for years when she had become pregnant. They decided to abort the baby. He drove her to the clinic to carry out this terrible act of selfishness. He dropped her off and she went in for the procedure. He didn't want to go in with her so he drove his car around for a while waiting for her to complete the task. At a certain point while driving around he felt a strong disturbing sensation. It was a deep grieving within his soul. He had never felt anything like it before or since. She came out later and was in a deep emotional state. They tried to console each other as best they could.

He also had another girlfriend years earlier who became pregnant. They agreed it was best to have an abortion. He didn't want his life complicated by a child. He admitted self-centeredness again was his reason for the abortion. He wishes now that he had talked his girlfriends into putting the babies up for adoption. Men are participants in abortion and guilty of a baby's death just as much as the women. Not always and in all circumstances but for the most part they're accomplices. If men would step up to the plate and encourage the woman to have their baby and let them know that they would be there to help, the woman would find the security she needs during her hormonal and physical changes that are happening within her, to have the baby.

Forgiveness is not only for murder by abortion, but for any type of murder. The Bible is full of repentant sinners who sought the forgiveness of God; the Apostle Paul and King David were accomplices to murder. We are all sinners in need of forgiveness. There are repentant murderers, adulterers, thieves, sexual perverts, gossips, jealous green-eyed monsters, gluttons, drunkards, drug abusers, coveters, etc. and our God of grace and mercy wants them to come to Jesus for the offer of forgiveness from sin, the forgiveness that salvation brings. We can't forgive ourselves as our sins are such an offense to our Creator. We need His forgiveness and His alone.

Helpful Ideas

♥ The Bible in the book of Jeremiah chapter 19 and in Leviticus chapter 20 talks about people sacrificing their children to false gods. We in America don't sacrifice our children to a religion of false gods, but we do sacrifice them for self, hence making ourselves into a false god. We must be thinking subconsciously "I'm god and I decide who lives!" Sadly, what is convenient for us turns out to be the most important consideration when it comes to deciding whether or not to allow a baby to live.

♥ **Write on a card Psalm 103:2-3:**
"Praise the Lord, my soul, and forget not all His benefits – Who forgives all your sins and heals all your diseases." (NIV)

♥ Remember, there is no sin too big or too horrific for God to forgive. He loves you even though you may feel unlovable. It may seem too good to be true, but trust God. He'll lift you up and remove all your sins.

♥ Pray that God leads you to the church He has in mind for you. Start looking around your neighborhood for churches and times of services. Start attending church within one to three weeks. Check out different churches until you find the loving Bible-centered church God is guiding you to. Also consider attending a midweek Bible study to gain more knowledge and maturity in godliness.

♥ When you find a church, remember that you are not better than the other members, nor are they better than you. We are all in need of God's mercy and grace. If some people in the church act standoffish and offensive, remember, we are all broken toys in need of fixing. Remain humble and loving and pray for the others. Don't let the haughty behavior of others chase you away from God. God wants you to go to church.

♥ **Meditate on Proverbs 16:18**

"Pride goes before destruction, and a haughty spirit before stumbling. It is better to be of a humble spirit with the lowly, than to divide the spoil with the proud." (NASB)

Vision of Jesus

This day started like any other ordinary day. My work schedule was from 10:00 a.m. to 8:00 p.m. It was a long work day so exercising was routine. A treadmill was set up in the hallway that led to the bathrooms with a light switch near the door. Walter, my second husband was leaving the hallway when he, not thinking about me in the middle of my exercise, turned off the light.

The darkness in a big industrial building was frightening initially. My first thought was to make my way safely off the machine and turn the light back on. Then a peace came over me and I decided to keep on exercising. After about ten minutes the vision began. Jesus appeared in a purple hue and I was in the palm of His right hand, comfy and cozy, looking up at Him smiling. I was perfectly safe and secure and He was about to tell and show me something I will never forget.

Without words He relayed this message to me: "Satan is attempting to attack you!" I saw Satan coming at me while I was in the right hand of the Lord. Jesus gently moved His left arm to cover me from Satan's attack. At that moment, I realized He did not act in violence with Satan. He slightly touched Satan and Satan went flying backwards with hands and feet flailing in the air. At the same time Jesus impressed upon me His pity for Satan. He did not want to hurt Satan, but He had to, in order to protect me, His child. That was the end of the vision.

Helpful Ideas

♥ We are not to act in any way that would show any allegiance to Satan, but we are to love and pity those who are being used by him. A tangible way of expressing our love to evil doers is to pray for them, especially praying for their salvation. I know I could not do this without God's help.

♥ It's difficult if not impossible to love someone who has hurt you intentionally. It's not in our human nature to react with love; however, it's our nature to react with anger, judgment and even sometimes hate. The key is to forgive others. We can't always do that on our own.

♥ When we give ourselves to God by knowing that Jesus Christ died on the cross for our sins and we humble ourselves and repent and make Jesus our Lord, you will then become a child of God, not just His creation. He forgives us, and we in turn, with His example, learn to forgive others.

♥ Also, it's important to completely accept God's forgiveness. It's not about forgiving yourself. Some people will go to a psychologist for years trying to learn how to forgive themselves and others, when in reality what we really need is to come to the realization that our forgiveness must come from God.

♥ You will be on the road to being set free when you realize that you are starting to love others more and more as your relationship with God deepens. Sometimes love for others is instantaneous and sometimes it's incremental. When it's incremental, don't be disappointed; eventually it will happen. Your heart will become a heart of love rather than a heart of hate when you ask God for help.

♥ The murderer David asked for God's help in Psalm 51.

Psalm 51:9-12 (TLB):

"Don't keep looking at my sins—erase them from your sight. Create in me a new, clean heart, O God, filled with clean thoughts and right desires. Don't toss me aside, banished forever from your presence. Don't take your Holy Spirit from me. Restore to me again the joy of your salvation, and make me willing to obey you."

♥ **Meditate on 1st John Chapter 3:23-24 (NASB):**

"And this is His commandment that we believe in the name of His Son Jesus Christ, and love one another, just as He commanded us. And the one who keeps His commandments abides in Him, and He in him. And we know by this that He abides in us, by the Spirit whom He has given us."

♥ **God tells His people in Ezekiel 36:26 (NIV)**

"I will give you a new heart and put a new spirit in you: I will remove from you your heart of stone and give you a heart of flesh."

♥ When you hear God speaking to your heart, you might want to write it down so that later you can think back on what He said. Remember it is only when you accept Jesus Christ as your Lord and Savior that the Holy Spirit will come to live permanently inside you. I know it sounds too good to be true, but it's true.

Dating and Marriage

This chapter starts off with a word of wisdom from the Bible which states:

"Do not smother the Holy Spirit. Do not scoff at those who prophesy, but test everything that is said to be sure it is true and if it is, then accept it." **(1st Thessalonians 5:19 – TLB)**

After Walters's death I was fifty-four years old, a widow who was lonely and wanting a husband. I decided to join dating services with a Christian affiliation. Presumably, the men I met would be interested in dating with marriage as their goal. That was not the case. The men I met through these dating sites were only interested in a self-absorbed good time and marriage seemed to far from their mind.

The last man I dated from one of these sites was someone that raised red warning signs, warnings that I should have taken more seriously at the time. This man had serious issues with honesty and integrity. His Jaguar was in the shop because someone had keyed it leaving a large scratch in the paint. He was upset that anyone would have the nerve to key "his" car.

I later realized it was probably someone he had previously been dating that keyed his car. The way he treated women, it was a wonder he didn't have his car keyed on a regular basis. He was interested in so many women at the same time that he would get mixed up on the phone and forget who he was talking to. So sad. That should have been warning enough about this man but apparently I needed more than that to help me recognize his game.

I had a dream vision regarding this man. I call it a "dream-vision" because it was a dream that was so real it was like a vision. We were standing in a doorway where everything was in an orange colored hew. This man was telling me that he loved me and to my surprise the Lord told me, "It's true, he does love you, but not like a man who could love you as a wife."

He came over later in the day after my dream-vision and I asked him to stop calling. I told him he was wasting my time because he was not interested in marriage. We said good bye to each other. He was a little surprised and asked "Why so fast? We just started dating. What's the rush?" I really had nothing to say at that point other than, "Goodbye." The Holy Spirit told me the truth about this relationship in the dream-vision and had set me free from this man and his unacceptable behavior. Know the truth and the truth will set you free.

At that time in my life I really didn't want to be bothered with someone who was not interested in marriage. My future husband was out there and I needed to find him, quickly, I'd hoped … before someone else did.

There was a dating site that had come to my attention that guaranteed six dates with reputable men. The service provided thorough background checks including a criminal records search, gainful employment or independent wealth with good credit standing, and most importantly to me, men interested in long term relationships leading to marriage. These six dates were guaranteed to take place within a two year period.

I went in for an interview. The woman who interviewed me sold me on the spot. She said, "You're cute and my clients will be excited to meet you and will appreciate you. I'm looking forward to working with you." No doubt she was looking forward to working with anyone willing to pay

$2,000 for six dates! Still, Mr. Wonderful would be worth it and I couldn't wait to pay the fee and sign the contract, which I did immediately.

After I left the office I was on my way to work when the Holy Spirit started laughing at me. He said, "Do you really think you have to pay for what I have for you?" I started laughing too. When the Holy Spirit laughs at me He always shares His humor with me and I laugh too. Now I was concerned about my $2,000 … hmmm.

That night while talking to my friends from work about the situation, one of the women told me about a free dating site. She said she had been dating her boyfriend for about two years and they had met on a free dating service called Plenty-of-Fish. She said that she had met other men on this site too, all nice guys. She insisted that I try it! The next day I went back to cancel the expensive dating service, got my $2,000 back and joined Plenty-of-Fish.

Owen, my current husband, and I met through this free dating site. On my profile I specified that I was looking for a "Fisher of Men." I figured that only a Christian who was interested in serving Christ would understand what this meant on my profile. **Matthew 4:19** *"come, follow me" Jesus said, "and I will make you fishers of men."* (Berean Bible).

As Christians we are called to lead lives of obedience and holiness made possible through the power of the Holy Spirit. A "Fisher of Men" would be pursuing holiness and obedience to Jesus. This was the kind of husband I was praying for.

About fifteen years earlier, I was sitting in the back seat of a minivan riding north on interstate five freeway from San Diego to Long Beach. We were going to a lawn party where there was going to be a jam session for musicians. At that time I was still with my former husband Walter. He was a professional drummer. We were driving with another couple and they were all sitting up front talking while I was in the back feeling left out because they were talking about things I did not understand. I had a book to occupy my time but at the moment I was looking out the window and daydreaming.

We were passing the Jenny Craig headquarters near the coastal beach town of Cardiff by the Sea when Walter made the comment to the effect that we owned stock in Jenny Craig's company. This was due to the fact that I had joined the organization several times. The Jenny Craig headquarters building is a wood structure with a unique design. It's not a building that you would drive by without noticing. The Holy Spirit spoke to me clearly as we passed the Jenny Craig Headquarters and told me to, "Pray for your future husband. He lives in this area and he needs prayer."

As odd as that seemed, I eagerly prayed for him at that moment and on into the future as well. As the years went by, I had forgotten about that incident. It wasn't until after Owen and I were married and talking about his conversion to Christ that I asked him if there was anyone who prayed for him to be saved. Owen said that he didn't know of anyone. That's when the Holy Spirit reminded me that I had prayed for him, all those years ago. I was humbled and grateful to God for allowing me the opportunity to pray for Owen even before I knew him. How wonderful of God to remind me of that incident. God does answer prayers!

Guess what? Owen was living in his house that was located in Cardiff by the Sea (which was the next exit right past the Jenny Craig headquarters building) during the time that I started praying for him years earlier!

Owen, at the age of sixty one years old, had never been married. I was surprised that he had never married since he was handsome and rugged looking. His personality is warm, and fun and he has a good dose of humility. Owen is also an unselfish person.

Owen mentioned to me that just before we met, the Holy Spirit was putting marriage on his heart too, so much so that he boldly proclaimed to his friends, "I'm getting married soon." He had prayed for a perfect woman for himself and for a lasting Godly marriage. About a month after that we met. And then three months later we were married! Praise the Lord.

Before marrying Owen I had just been through a marriage that I thought was ideal until after Walter died. The secrets of one affair after another that Walter engaged in during our marriage were finally revealed. I was broken and crushed beyond help. Because of this unfaithfulness of Walter, I became extremely jealous and needy. Owen said that "my love and God's love together would overcome my problems and this love would eventually heal me." Troubles were plenty right from the start of our marriage but love is binding and strong and in the end Owen was right. Love did heal my broken heart and our broken start.

Owen's brother and sister-in-law were going through a break-up when Owen and I started dating. We were totally enthralled with each other and we were about to have our first disagreement. We were sitting in Owen's van in a parking lot near a place where we had just had a cup of coffee. It was a fancy place. Owen told me he considers whatever environment he's in as his living room, comfortable, safe and secure wherever he goes. I'm the opposite. There is not a place in this world that feels like my living room other than my very own living room. However, we were comfortable sitting there in his van talking.

Owen was a disc jockey and had a van so that he could carry his DJ equipment. He'd been a DJ for thirty years. The van was one of those vans that doesn't have windows on the sides, the kind that looks spooky and suspicious. It was a working van he said; his equipment was more secure without windows. I found cd's he had made for other women, make-up, hair pins and everything that indicated there had been plenty of women making themselves at home in this van. Grrrrr!

At that time I worked the night shift and later in the day, at home, I slept then back to work I would go. While sitting in the van I sweetly asked Owen, "What are you doing tonight?" Owen told me, he was going to have dinner and visit with his sister-in-law. I looked at Owen like he must be out of his mind. "You mean the sister-in-law that is now a single woman? You're going to go hang out with a single woman while I'm sleeping and working? I don't think so! How would you like it if while you're busy working I go hang out with a single man?"

I was furious and was adamant that he cancel his dinner plans on the spot. He called his sister-in-law right then and canceled. This was the first incident of contention we would have over the next several years. I was appeased for the moment, but it seemed like we were in two different worlds attempting to cross a vast expanse to reach each other. We needed God's help desperately.

I didn't understand why Owen smiled and waved back at women walking down the sidewalk or hooted and hollered when he appreciated a talented female performer. I thought clapping should be enough. I didn't understand when Owen was still using his ex-girlfriend's name as his password for a bank account. I was disturbed with his three thousand plus e-mails, some from women he had known in the past.

I certainly didn't understand when we went out to dinner with another couple and his attention was at the next table all during dinner. The woman at that table kept looking at Owen and of course he kept looking back. I was hurt, furious and wondering what I was doing trying to hang on to a man who was so insensitive and out of touch with appropriate marital behavior. He later claimed he was looking at a man that looked just like his brother's neighbor and for some reason he found that a very curious thing. I felt it was disrespectful and embarrassing to me, we fought about it for days.

About a month later a similar situation happened to me at a different restaurant and there was a man staring at me and I was looking back at him. Owen asked me what was going on and I told him, "That man over there is staring at me and I'm a little uncomfortable." It was only then that Owen told me, "Now you know how it feels to be stared at and staring back at someone at a different table." I told Owen my response was not the same because I told the truth immediately and did not try to hide and act like it hadn't happen. Had Owen told me the truth from the beginning we may not have had to stay up day and night fighting about it … then again we may have.

After being single for 61 years Owen was only doing what came naturally to him. He didn't think there was anything outrageous about his behavior. He thought this disturbance had to be about my Hispanic heritage. He'd always understood Hispanic women were jealous and that I was no exception. His last girlfriend had been Hispanic and I supposed she was disturbed for the same reason. No surprise there!

It was far worse than all this. I did not want Owen looking at any women anywhere or talking to women or even recognizing that the female population existed! This was foreign to Owen since his whole life had been about dating and interacting with women up to this point. My jealousy was bazaar and abnormal; neither Owen nor I knew how to resolve the problem. Being the typical male, he wanted our problems solved and solved yesterday. This was beyond what he'd envisioned as "Marriage." He was heartbroken, he'd waited his whole life to get married to the "Right" person and now that the right person did not seem to be so "Right."

To add insult to injury I was going through menopause, and that stage in a woman's life does not lend itself to patience and understanding; quite the opposite in fact. When we did have our storms they sometimes lasted for days on end and it seems as though we had them weekly. We'd stay up all night fighting and struggling over our unfulfilled expectations. According to Owen I was the problem and he was at a breaking point. Because of our situation he cried out to God for help one day, "What else can I do God? I have nothing left. Help me or I can't go on with this marriage."

It was after this crying out in desperation to God that God answered Owen. God often answers us when we're at the end of ourselves and we can't go on without Him. He tells us exactly that in the Bible when He says in Jeremiah 29:13, *"You will seek me and find me when you seek me with all your heart."* Owen cried out to God with all his heart. It was then that God showed Owen the depth of emotional turmoil and trauma that I had been through to bring me to this point of borderline insanity. God said to Owen's heart "This isn't all about you Owen. You are to be her hero. That's what you always wanted: To find a woman to be a hero to and marry her, so here is your chance.

I've given you this opportunity to grow in selflessness. If you had been through all that your wife had been through all these years you may not have it altogether either. So be a hero!"

The Lord showed Owen what it would take to be a good husband to God's special daughter. God gave Owen a deeper love and compassion for me. Deeper than any love he'd ever known. The kind of love and compassion that allowed Owen to lay down his life on my behalf, which makes sense as Jesus tells us in Ephesians 5:25 *"For husbands, this means love your wives, just as Christ loved the church, He gave up His life for her."*

Owen is a servant of love for me as I am for him. I needed his selfless love to heal. I also asked God for a man that would love me. God told me, "He'll only be capable of loving you if he loves me enough." Because Owen does love God with all his heart, he is a trustworthy man and capable of loving me. I'm now able to lead a more normal life. Owen and I could not have this beautiful marriage if we did not forgive each other for our past mistakes, the intentional and unintentional mistakes. Forgiveness is a huge part of being in God's will.

Helpful Ideas

- ♥ Rest assured that God wants to communicate with you. God cares about every aspect of your life. Ask Him to reveal Himself to you and He will. It's God's will for you to have a real relationship with Him; He created you for that very purpose. Expect it, live in it and thank Him for it.

- ♥ Start talking to God. It's called prayer. Learn to listen. As you mature in Christ you will become more sensitive to the leadings of the Holy Spirit in your life. God will reveal Himself to you more often because of your increased capacity to hear. The best way I have of describing how I hear God is likened to spiritual telepathy. My mind understands what He is saying and He's communicating clearly and concisely through words that are not spoken audibly but through my inner consciousness. Communing with God.

♥ If you read the Bible you will find that God was talking to people over and over again. God has not changed. He loves us, the people He created.

♥ When you read the following Scriptures believe that God is talking to you personally because He is. Dwell on these Scriptures and make them your truth.

Jeremiah 29:11 (MSG)
For I know the plans that I have for you, says the Lord. They are plans for good and not for evil, to give you a future and a hope.

Matthew 6:8 (ASV)
For your Father knows what things you have need of, before you ask Him.

Philippians 4:6 (NIV)
Do not be anxious about anything, but in every situation, by prayer and petition, with thanksgiving, present your requests to God.

1st John 5:14 (NIV)
This is the confidence we have in approaching God; that if we ask anything according to His will He hears us.

Acts 13:52 (NASB)
And the disciples were continually filled with joy and with the Holy Spirit.

♥ Remember no matter what our need is, God already knows what it is. And if it is in His good and perfect will, He will answer our prayers in His own perfect way and time.

♥ There are hundreds upon hundreds of God's promises in the Bible. These promises are mentioned throughout the Bible. When we fully understand, believe and put them into practice, they bring us lasting peace. A peace that the nonbelievers would not understand.

A wonderful result of this peace is that it allows us to have lasting joy. A joy that the ungodly world doesn't understand. Here is how it works. God's truth heals our minds. Truth makes our minds think orderly and correctly. God's truth comes to set us free and gives us lasting mental health. His healing truths bring mental orderliness and finally lasting peace. We can't have lasting joy without peace. Ultimately, salvation is our source of mental health. Salvation is trusting in Jesus Christ as our Savior. It brings us to God's truth which brings lasting peace which is crowned by lasting joy.

♥ The opposite is also true; lies create insanity and disorder. This causes our thoughts to be out of touch with reality so we are thinking disorderly and incorrectly. Chaos comes from lies and there is no peace when mental chaos is in our minds. It depresses us and can cause all sorts of unwanted behavior, frustrations and anger.

Cardiff By The Sea

Trusting God is not easy when things are not going our way or what we believe is best. Such was the case when Owen wanted his ex-girlfriend, her daughter and son to remain in his house when we were about to get married. Owen's house was in foreclosure at the time and he wanted to let it go. I wanted his ex-girlfriend and her children out at all costs. He insisted I invite her to our wedding, which I did. Fortunately she had the decency and common sense to decline and not show up.

When Owen stopped supporting the ex-girlfriend's unstable life style and taking care of her children, she finally found work, something she tried to avoid for fifteen years. Owen was grateful that he was able to help raise those children during their impressionable years. When I came along I felt it was time for Owen to end their relationship. This was difficult for all of us because they had become a dysfunctional family of sorts. If she had a crisis she wanted Owen to stop whatever he was doing and resolve the problem. At that time I was too broken to handle any relationship with an ex-girlfriend or her children. I wanted none of it!

I was learning that the Christian life was not a life without difficulties, but it was a life with a God who would never leave us nor forsake us in our difficulties. With the stress of my job and being quite concerned about finances, I asked Owen to have his ex-girlfriend, her children and others who were living in his house to move out. My house that I lived in was in a poor neighborhood, although it was a nice house on a cul-de-sac and newer compared to others in the community at large. I thought we should rent it out or sell it and get his house out of foreclosure with the proceeds.

Owen's house was in a fancy part of town and was a good investment with an ocean view. Also, as his new wife, I thought I deserved to live there rather than his ex-girlfriend and her children. I was stubborn about this to the point that we had to take them to court, forcing them to move when they would not leave voluntarily. They had lived there rent free for over a year and in my mind that was enough.

Owen loved her children and had been raising one of them from birth. In Owen's mind, asking them to leave was like putting them on the street and contributing to their homelessness. He had been supporting her lifestyle for so many years she was dependent on Owen. In the past, Owen had made it a point to base his relationships on the fact that the children were his main priority. I didn't have children and this situation was not sitting well with me. Owen and I went round and round over this dilemma. It was not pretty. In fact, to this day I'm surprised our relationship survived. I know it would not have survived without God's gracious intervention.

We had just come from court requesting an eviction for the people living in Owen's house which included the ex and her children and a couple other roommates. Owen had rented out rooms to a myriad of people throughout the years, and not all had been paying rent. Calling some of them tenants was a stretch. The judge said we could not remove the people living in his house, and I was furious. That night I could not sleep and when I can't sleep I pray.

In the wee hours of the morning in my cozy living room I prayed with all the sincerity that my stony heart could muster. I asked God, "You own the whole wide world. Why do you have to let those people live in that house?" God answered with sternness and said, "It is true what you say. I do own the whole world and everything in it. What business is it of yours where I let these people live?" At that moment I understood that God was taking care of these people the same way He was taking care of me. After all, Owen and I had a home. God was telling me to mind my own business. Ouch! I was still not happy that they were in his house; however, I had a peace and acceptance about the situation that I would never have had without that word from God and God's discipline to put me in my place. Prior to the Lord speaking to me I had been frustrated out of my mind. Owen will confirm this! I was doing my best to frustrate Owen out of his mind too.

Not long afterwards his house was put up for auction. The new owner took possession and actually tore down the house and built a large two story house in its place.

Helpful Ideas

♥ God tells us that, *"My thoughts are not your thoughts, Nor are your ways My ways"* (Isaiah 55:8-9 NKJV). He talks to us and shares with us His thoughts when we go to Him in prayer. The Bible also tells us that, *"Those whom the Lord loves, He disciplines, and He scourges every son whom He receives"* (Hebrews 12:6 NASB). It is a wonderful thing to be disciplined by the Lord, for even while we're undergoing His disciplining, the tremendous love He has for us is stunning. When He asked me, "What business is it of yours?" it was unpleasant. It was a rebuke from a caring parent; as a child of God He was teaching me how to respond correctly. It's not easy. The Bible says in **1 Corinthians 13:11 (NLT)**:

When I was a child, I spoke and thought and reasoned as a child. But when I grew up, I put away childish things.

It's not easy for us as adults to put away childish understanding, thinking and speaking. We are selfish by nature and the Holy Spirit has some serious work to do within us, but thankfully the Holy Spirit is up to the task.

♥ There is nothing better than to be loved by God. God loves you right now, right where you're at in the midst of anything that is going on in your life. Ask Him to forgive you for your sins in the name of Jesus. Read His love letter, the Bible, and let Jesus become the Lord of your heart and life. There is nothing more wonderful in the world than being aware of the love God has for us. He already loves you but until you accept His son Jesus as your Lord and Savior, you're not able to comprehend the depths of that love. When you come to salvation in Jesus, God freely gives you His Holy Spirit to live inside you and guide you. Salvation is your choice, it's free and the Holy Spirit is available now.

♥ Remember, in order to love someone, you have to get to know that person. The same is true as you get to know God; your love for Him will grow. Study all of the characteristics and expectations of God the Father, God the Son Jesus, and God the Holy Spirit. Read the Bible daily. Jot down the scriptures that jump out at you and personally speak to your heart.

♥ If you would come to God, He will help you through whatever difficult situation you're going through. He'll commune with you and bring you peace. Talk to Him in prayer, then take some quiet time and listen for any of His leadings and obey.

Suggestion

Pray the Lord's Prayer found in Mathew 6:9-13 and read it slowly part by part. Do your best to understand what Jesus was saying to the Father.

Life Saver

Owen and I are "Fishers of Men," which simply means we make a concerted effort to share with others how much God loves them and how they need salvation. We go fishing for lost souls by placing audio CDs on the door handles of cars, trucks and vans in parking lots. The CDs instruct people convincingly as to why they should believe in Jesus Christ as their Lord and Savior, and how to live a life that is pleasing to God. It teaches unbelievers the benefits of trusting in Christ for salvation and how to go about doing that. We travel around the country with the specific intention of going where the Holy Spirit leads us. We believe someone somewhere may be desperate and in need of hearing from the Lord, and this may be one way in which the Lord will be able to reach that person.

"Hon, let's go and deliver some Love Letter CDs," I told Owen. "That sounds good," he said. "Where should we go to deliver them?" We decided to drive north up the Oregon coast towards Astoria from our little oasis in Southern Oregon. Prior to any major trip we usually wash the van. I clean the inside while Owen washes the outside.

I was still cleaning the inside when Owen finished the outside. He decided to go water the garden. About 30 feet below our driveway is our garden. Below our garden and down a steep cliff is the river. As Owen was watering the garden, he heard a loud helicopter hovering over the river. This was an unusual event for us since we live out in the woods. Any aircraft flying in this area is rare. We had never seen or heard a low flying helicopter anywhere in the area before. Owen described it as being very loud with the blades of the chopper rotating and swooshing like in the movies when a chopper lands in a war zone. Scary!

Owen thought it might have landed down by the river on our property because the sound was loud and steady. He thought it might have been a life flight rescuing someone. He was yelling and waving his hands to get my attention. I was still inside the van and didn't hear a thing. He was about to walk down to the river to investigate when the sound abruptly stopped and never returned ... strange!

When I got out of the van a few minutes later he asked me if I heard the helicopter. I hadn't heard a thing. The windows had been closed to keep the water out of the van while Owen was washing it and after he had finished I hadn't bothered to open them. I was disappointed that I hadn't heard it and asked Owen why he didn't let me know what was happening. He said he tried but was caught up in the moment and didn't think to hike up to the driveway to get me. It struck me as odd that his reaction was so out of character. He was disturbed because as loud as the helicopter had been he didn't see it and the noise had stopped just as abruptly as it had started.

Later in the day when Owen was working in the yard painting a shed he had just built, he had a strange feeling that he was painting the shed for someone else to enjoy. He felt that we were about to experience a tragedy of some sort and never enjoy what he was building. He wondered why he would think such a thing. Eventually he came to the conclusion that it was just a negative thought and shrugged it off. Later I went into the house to do some work and a strong impression came upon me that I would not be returning to this house. It was a disturbing thought.

That evening Owen and I were in our office duplicating the evangelistic audio CDs. Owen heard what sounded like a crash down by the river. I was in the same room and he asked, "Do you hear that?" "No," I said. He told me to come to the window and listen. Still I heard nothing while he was hearing the sound of what he now described as metal grinding and being pulled over the river bed rocks. I was disappointed because I heard nothing. We were both perplexed.

That night, Owen and I went to bed after saying our prayers and said goodnight to each other. We drifted off to what Owen and I call our other life, sleep. Then the nightmare started. In my dream I remembered our van was rolling over and over. So I reached out to hold on to Owen. His back was to me and he would not respond. This startled me as Owen never hesitates to help me.

The van was rolling over and I was screaming in total turmoil and Owen wouldn't respond. That was most disturbing to me, Owen not responding. When a wife is used to being pampered and loved by her husband there is nothing more devastating than the absence of that loving care and attention. The van finally stopped rolling over and was scraping and sliding on pavement. I was thinking we're going to be okay now as the momentum of the van was slowing.

Suddenly there was no sound and we were suspended in a silent, motionless and safe place for just a moment. While that moment lingered the realization came to me that we had gone over a cliff and we were about to come crashing down onto the rocks and into a river. After the impact I knew a helicopter would be coming for me. I was injured and would never be the same again and worse yet, Owen was dead and gone. I didn't know where I was going to live and who would help me.

Truthfully, it was not like any dream I've ever had; it was more like a vision. I immediately woke up and then understood all the Lord had been trying to tell us for the past twenty-four hours. Lying in bed that morning I asked Owen if we could cancel the trip we had been planning. It was then that Owen and I began talking and sharing information with each other about what had been going on. We both realized what the Holy Spirit had been trying to tell us.... "Don't take this trip!"

While Owen and I were talking, he remembered another thought impression he had. "There's going to be a wreck and it won't be your fault. It will involve another driver, a young man, who has no intention of hurting you." That additional information illuminated why he was not going to enjoy the work he had put into the shed. It became obvious that all these warning thoughts were the still small voice of the Holy Spirit. He was telling us in different ways: audio sounds of the helicopter and metal dragging on rocks, thought impressions of us not coming back to this house, and then the grand finale of the dream which depicted the events as they would occur. These all had been warnings to not take the trip. Finally we knew, after all this that the trip was not God's plan for us.

We were absolutely convinced that God spared our lives and we were in awe of our blessed Savior's mercy.

Helpful Ideas

- ♥ It's God's will to communicate with us if we will but listen. The Holy Spirit is with people and if we are born again unto salvation through Jesus, the Holy Spirit is actually living inside of us and is always ready to counsel us. We need to welcome Him to do just that and then listen for His direction, warnings and help.

- ♥ Scripture reading from the Berean Literal Bible: **Acts 2:17**

  "And it will be in the last days, God says, I will pour out of My Spirit upon all flesh, and your sons and your daughters will prophesy, and your young men will see visions, and your elders will dream dreams."

♥ Think about **Psalm 91:14-16.** It's one of God's many wonderful promises to us. This is from the New Living Translation:

The Lord says, "I will rescue those who love me. I will protect those who trust in my name. When they call on me, I will answer; I will be with them in trouble. I will rescue and honor them. I will reward them with a long life and give them my salvation."

♥ Identify the most troubling situation in your life. Once you've made that identification, take it to God in prayer. Let God know what it is that's bothering you specifically about the situation. Then ask Him to share with you His thoughts on the matter. Ask Him to adjust your mind and give you the wisdom to rethink the situation with His wisdom. Ask Him to resolve the situation for you. Then start thanking Him every day for His answer. Learn to trust Him and learn to listen.

♥ Read Psalm 23 several times a day for a week or two. Tell God you love Him even if you don't know Him that well yet. The more you get to know God through His word in the Bible and sermons you hear, the more you will come to love Him.

♥ **(Jeremiah 1:5 NIV)**
Before I formed you in the womb I knew you, before you were born I set you apart.

God was specifically speaking to Jeremiah in this passage, however, the same truth can be said of us too. He knows us even better than we know ourselves.

♥ **Psalm 139:13-14 (NIV)**
For you created my inmost being; you knit me together in my mother's womb. I praise you because I am fearfully and wonderfully made; your works are wonderful, I know that full well.

Here King David was acknowledging what God had said to him, again it can be said of you and me as well. He knows us inside and out and loves us anyway. Trust Him.

The Cave

Owen led a charmed life. That's the way I see it looking from the outside. His Dad was an Air Force war hero who flew combat missions during World War Two. He was a dad who would talk to Owen and share with him about what is right and wrong. They had a loving relationship. This was impressive to me since a loving, communicative relationship with my dad was not my reality. Owen has a picture of himself when he was quite young, leaning up against his dad's knee – you can see the trust and love they shared. It showed that this parent-child relationship was a very healthy one. That is the way God meant it to be. It's a beautiful picture and one I keep in my jewelry box on my dresser so that I may look at it periodically. For some reason that picture brings peace to my heart.

Owen describes his Mom as Donna Reed from the "Donna Reed Show" mixed with Marie from "Everybody Loves Raymond" all wrapped up in one. She is a nurturing and loving mother who also had a career. She grew up in Los Angeles. Owen was born in North Hollywood. She was a glamorous woman with a job like the beautiful Della Street on "Perry Mason." She water-skied, danced, sang and had a full and rounded life. She loved her little boy with all the love God puts in a mother's heart. Owen was the only child for the first twelve years of their marriage.

To me, on the outside looking in, Owen's life was blessed. Owen's mom also read to him from the Bible on Sunday mornings during his grammar school years.

Owen had neighbors with a swimming pool and they would not let Owen come and swim as often as he would have liked. So Owen's parents had a pool built for him! Then at the age of twelve Owen realized he wanted a little brother very much.

God must have heard Owen's request because his parents were surprised when Owen's request came to fruition shortly thereafter. Owen's parents would move the world for him, their world anyway. He was loved and showered in love by God, parents, grandparents, neighbors and friends.

During his earlier years Owen's parents would take him to his Grandma Pauline's most weekends. Grandpa Wesley would take Owen to the store and let him pick a toy and they'd come home to root beer floats, popcorn and watching shows like "My Three Sons" and the "Honeymooners" and then it was off to bed. We have a darling picture up on the wall of Owen when he was about seven years old with Grandpa Wesley's cowboy boots and hat on. Little Owen is taking a pose shooting the enemy with his Grandpa's big six gun pulled out from his holster.

As Owen matured into adulthood he became very influenced by worldly things. Although he didn't know it at the time, his life was becoming worldly, prideful and centered around the need to be liked, loved, and seeking respect from others. Eventually he became self-absorbed and grew spiritually empty inside, and yet the world would have seen a successful handsome bachelor who owned his beautiful ocean view home with fancy cars and beautiful women who loved him and would have married him had he asked. He, like most of us, searched for the meaning of life and love in all the wrong places. The following vision of Jesus was seen by Owen. I'll let Owen describe it:

"In my effort to satisfy my cravings for self-satisfaction and living for my worldly lusty pleasures I got into drugs, alcohol and partying and all that comes with it. The rule became 'Live it up,' especially if all I'm going to have is lights out at the end of my life. Also getting high was a way for me to numb myself of having to think about anything too serious, especially my future.

"This lifestyle, in time, led me to more dissatisfaction, more emptiness and now actual harm to my body and mind. After years of living like this, one night I had a dream. In this short powerful dream which was really more than a dream, it was very real … In this dream I was walking down a dirt path towards a cave and a friend of mine was in the cave with drugs and as I was headed toward the cave entrance to get high with my friend Rick, I noticed a boulder off to my left about ten feet away.

"I took a second look and then the rock turned into a moving holographic image of Jesus Christ. It shocked me and I couldn't take my eyes off of Him. I stopped dead in my tracks and noticed He was frowning at me. His eyes and entire presence was penetrating and His head was slightly moving from left to right in disapproval of what I was about to do with my friend. I felt like I was disappointing Jesus very much, so I turned and yelled to Rick, "I'm not coming in, I'm going home." All in an effort to please Jesus.

"So I turned around and looked again at Jesus now over my right shoulder and noticed that He was sort of smiling and slightly nodding his head affirmatively. I suddenly woke up from this vision quite startled. Like I said it was more than a dream and I will never forget the impact of seeing Jesus' face and what it meant.

"That following Sunday I went to a local church for the first time since I became an adult. The Pastor was preaching, to my surprise (now knowing it was not a coincidence), a sermon that seemed to be a sermon just for me and about my personal struggles. This sermon started to reveal the truth and understanding for the meaning of life. It exposed just how an empty, self-centered and worldly life eventually leads to nothing good. He asked if there was anyone who wanted to change their life and give it to Jesus Christ. I volunteered with tears streaming out of my eyes. I prayed that Jesus would take away my emptiness and give my life meaning. I also asked Him to take away my past sins and for Jesus to become my Lord and Savior for the rest of my life.

"From that day forward bit by bit, I began to commit myself to discovering what Jesus was all about. This included, of course, His teachings and how they apply to my daily life. Marvelous internal and outward changes, especially in my attitude, took place and it still continues to improve. No more drugs, alcohol, cussing, nothing X or even R rated to look at or listen to. Seeking to separate myself from sin, this change for good took time and each year I could look back and see that it has become better.

"Even selfishness and pride are dissolving. Life did not become boring at all without these sins. Life each year becomes more satisfying and turns out to be more genuine. The blessings keep pouring out. My wife and I walk close with Jesus and it's such a wonderful changed life. Jesus truly is a Savior!!! We try to tell others **not to reject** the loving hand of Jesus reaching out to the lost. And whatever you do, please come to salvation; otherwise your biggest problem in life has not been solved.

"Your biggest problem in life is this; do not have this life on earth come to an end without Jesus forgiving your life-long sin debt. Don't take the risk of on your last day finding yourself standing before a perfect, holy and just God with your unholy sin debt unforgiven by Jesus. It will be your personal judgment day. Sin cannot go unpunished, otherwise God would not be perfectly just or even good. Salvation in Christ will cancel your guilty verdict and bring you safely into heaven and cancel your trip to hell.

"Do what I did and go find a Christ-centered loving church that teaches directly out of the Bible. Go up to the pastor at some point and tell him you want to give your life to Jesus and follow Jesus' teachings for the rest of your life. Start reading the New Testament in the Bible, especially John, Ephesians and Luke to get a grasp on your new life in Christ. There is unending joy and security in Jesus' salvation. He died for you and paid the ultimate price so that you may live with Him in Heaven for eternity."

Helpful Ideas

The following scriptures taken out of the Bible will match up with Owen's testimony.

♥ **1 John 3:8 (NIV)**
The one who does what is sinful is of the devil, because the devil has been sinning from the beginning. The reason the Son of God appeared was to destroy the devil's work.

♥ **Proverbs 3:7 (NLT)**
Don't be impressed with your own wisdom. Instead, fear the Lord and turn away from evil.

♥ **John 3:19-20 (NIV)**
This is the verdict: Light has come into the world, but people loved darkness instead of light because their deeds were evil. [20] Everyone who does evil hates the light, and will not come into the light for fear that their deeds will be exposed.

♥ **Mark 8:36 (NLT)**
And what do you benefit if you gain the whole world but lose your own soul?

♥ **Romans 2:12 (NLT)**
Do not copy the behavior and customs of this world, but let God transform you into a new person by changing the way you think. Then you will learn to know God's will for you, which is good and pleasing and perfect.

♥ **1 John 2:16 (NLT)**
For the world offers only a craving for physical pleasure, a craving for everything we see, and pride in our achievements and possessions. These are not from the Father, but are from this world.

♥ **Ephesians 2:3 (NASB)**
... we too all formerly lived in the lusts of our flesh, indulging the desires of the flesh and of the mind, and were by nature the children of wrath, even as the rest.

♥ **Ephesians 1:7 (NKJV)**
In Him [Jesus] we have redemption through His blood, the forgiveness of our sins, according to the riches of His grace.

♥ **Ephesians 1:18 (NIV)**
I pray that the eyes of your heart may be enlightened in order that you may know what is the hope of His calling, what are the riches of the glory of His inheritance in His holy ones.

♥ **John 3:16 (NKJV)**
For God so loved the world that He gave His only begotten Son, that whoever believes in Him should not perish, but have everlasting life.

♥ **Philippians 4:7-8 (NIV)**
And the peace of God, which transcends all understanding, will guard your hearts and your minds in Christ Jesus. Finally, brothers and sisters, whatever is true, whatever is noble, whatever is right, whatever is pure, whatever is lovely, whatever is admirable—if anything is excellent or praiseworthy—think about such things.

♥ People spend years going to other people for counseling with a yearning for peace of mind and emotions. People spend years in prison longing for peace, wondering how it all went so wrong. Some people spend a lifetime searching for answers and longing for peace. If you're going through a tough time, peace is what you need. Jesus Christ is the Prince of Peace.

♥ **Read Isaiah 9:6**
For to us a child is born, to us a son is given, and the government will be on his shoulders. And he will be called Wonderful Counselor, Mighty God, Everlasting Father, Prince of Peace.

♥ One final thought for this chapter; you are not called to go through this life alone. Jesus promised you a Helper, a Comforter, a Truth Bearer, who will be with you forever, that is the Holy Spirit. He will remind you of all truth in the word of God, but it is incumbent upon you to read and study the Bible so that the Holy Spirit of Truth can bring the truth to you when you need it most. The truth in the word of God is the truth the Holy Spirit uses. He will not stray from the word of God.

♥ Remember that God knows all about every choice you've ever made and He still loves you and always will, regardless of whether the choices you made were good or bad. Remember, until you accept Jesus Christ as your Lord and Savior, your biggest problem in life is unresolved. Separation from God is hell and it will be a frightening place to spend eternity. This is not what God wants for you. You are precious in His sight. There's a prayer at the end of this book, chapter twenty, that you may pray with sincerity asking Jesus for salvation. It's that simple. God is not interested in making this hard for us. He loves us and always will. Also go to church on Sunday and at the end of the service, if they give a call go forward and accept Jesus Christ as your Savior, do it! Another option is to go up to the Pastor at the end of the service and tell him you want the Salvation that Jesus offers. He'll know what you're asking for and will help you.

Page Arizona

A year after Owen and I were married we began to think of moving away from San Diego (the city was too full of our past personal history). Owen was a life-long bachelor for sixty plus years with a girlfriend story around every corner, or so I thought. I had been married for twenty-eight years when my second husband, Walter, passed away from lung cancer. All of those years were spent in San Diego. Our new marriage needed a fresh start.

At the time I wasn't ready to retire so we decided to move to some place where I could get a job. Owen said he needed to be near water, which was not an issue for me. I understood his fixation for water as his parents had a pool built for him when he was seven. He started waterskiing at the age of twelve and then surfing in his late teens and continued surfing into his mid-fifties.

We thought about Lake Powell by Page, Arizona as a possibility. I searched for a possible government job in that town and there was an opening as a 911 operator at Lake Powell. I had been working as a 911 operator as well as a police and fire dispatcher for about ten years.

This new 911 job at Lake Powell was inviting. I was intrigued with how the dispatchers found people without addresses during an emergency on and around the lake. Working on a lake with no addresses was something new. With only cell phone capability to pin point a location it seemed that it could be difficult. During a 911 phone call the most important information is location. When answering the phone on an emergency call we say, "911, Where is your emergency?" I remember the trainers stressing, "Location, Location, Location!"

I was offered the position right after the interview. I asked for a day to talk to my husband and think about the offer. We needed time to pray as this was a big decision to move to northern Arizona. She agreed. Owen and I drove around town looking at houses within our price range. Our price range left us with not much to look at. Nothing impressive. We went out that evening for a Chinese dinner. It's difficult to find anything negative to say about Kung Pao Chicken, and yet the café was old and dusty. We ended the evening with a fun game of bowling. Owen thought he was going to impress me with a great score. Not! We both hadn't bowled in years and it showed. Regardless of the lack of skill, we had a great time.

We talked throughout the day regarding the pros and cons and of our desire to live in this town. The town was not impressive, especially during the drab winter season. The lake was cold and dreary. It definitely was a summer vacation town where people go to enjoy the massive lake, creating the need for 911 operators due to boating mishaps.

We went to bed that evening in a comfy motel. In the middle of the night we both woke up at the same time with an evil foreboding. We both had a sense of deep loneliness, isolation and evil all wrapped up in one ugly package. We looked at each other and said, "Let's get the heck out of here!" I called the kind lady who offered me the job the next day while driving out of town to let her know I had decided to decline the job offer and thanked her. We are so happy that we now live in Oregon and not in Page Arizona!

God wants to communicate with us before we make mistakes, if we will allow Him that opportunity. We always try to allow the Holy Spirit to guide us and to be open to all the ways He does that. There are circumstances that arise where we need God's specific direction. For instance, the 911 job, was that God's direction for me at that time in my life? Was this the right location? No, it wasn't. God directed my husband and I in the middle of the night at the same time by waking us and speaking to our spirit to move along. This was not coincidental that we woke up at the same time in the middle of the night with that same dread. God communicates with us however He chooses. He will never tell us to do anything that is contrary to His word. It's important to read the Bible and get a firm grasp of its content. We need to always ask the Holy Spirit to help us. Ask for wisdom and patience then wait on the Lord.

Helpful Ideas

♥ **Proverbs 16:9 (TLB)**
   We should make plans – counting on God to direct us.

   Another version, the New American Standard Bible (NASB) says it this way:

   The mind of man plans his way, but the Lord directs his steps.

   Still another version, The Message Bible (MSG), says:

   We plan the way we want to live, but only God makes us able to live it.

♥ Life presents a host of variables such as how to earn a living, where we work, who we date, who we marry, what house we buy, etc. … all choices that God is happy to counsel us in if we will wait on Him and ask Him for His help and guidance. Pray.

♥ It's vitally important to know the Bible because the wisdom in the Bible can guide your decision making process. For instance the Bible says do not be unequally yoked, meaning don't date someone who does not love and obey God, and if you do, then expect the challenges that go with that unwise decision. Don't attempt to make money dishonestly when the Bible says *"Do Not Steal."*

♥ Do not make things more important than God. I know it's tempting to believe that God no longer guides human beings and that He only did so in the Bible times, but that is not true. If it were, Jesus would not tell us in Revelation 3:20, *"Behold, I stand at the door and knock; if anyone hears My voice and opens the door, I will come in to him, and will dine with him, and he with Me."* Why would He say such a thing if He did not intend to communicate with us? He wouldn't. Men become pastors of churches and they are and should be counseled and led by God ... How does this happen if God does not communicate with them? **"My sheep hear my voice, and I know them, and they follow me,"** says the Lord in **John 10:27**. How can you have a relationship with God if communication isn't a two-way street? Yes, there are many times God remains silent, but not always. God does as He chooses. A darkness had enveloped Owen and I that night at the same time and to ignore that type of communication would have been unwise. The Bible is the compass that will guide us in most of life's decisions, however, there are situations that arise that are personal and not specifically in the Bible, like the job in Page. It is God's will for us to work; however, where we work is a variable.

♥ **Read Exodus Chapter 20**, The Ten Commandments. Then read **1st and 2nd Thessalonians**. Eventually read the entire New Testament. Read as much as the Holy Spirit guides you to read each day. It could be as little as one scripture you jot on a card and carry in your pocket, reading it throughout the day. It could be as much as 3 chapters or more. What is important is to read the Bible every day.

♥ We should think in terms of God as a parent, which He is, our Heavenly Father; parents don't want to have to make decisions for their adult children, but they do like to be consulted for advice. Parents do not like to be ignored, nor does God. It's best to ask Him for guidance; that helps to avoid needless suffering in the future. Be advised, I didn't say we would avoid suffering, but needless suffering. After all we're not in Heaven yet, but when you become a saved Christian, you're on your way!

♥ Much of the time when our parents leave this earth they leave a will and if you are interested in your inheritance, which anyone would be, you'll read the will. God said in **Ephesians 1:5**, **"He predestined us to adoption as sons through Jesus Christ to Himself,"** and He left us an inheritance as explained in the Bible.

♥ An acronym that is common for the Bible is

Basic
Instructions
Before
Leaving
Earth

♥ **Romans 8:14-15 (NLT)**
For all who are being led by the Spirit of God are children of God. So you have not received a spirit that makes you fearful slaves. Instead you received God's Spirit when He adopted you as His own children. Now we call Him, "Abba! Father!"

♥ **2 Thessalonians 3: 16 (NLT)**
Now may the Lord of peace Himself give you His peace at all times and in every situation.

Disobedience

Owen and I were planning to go into town to pick-up supplies and to fill the truck with gas. The Holy Spirit impressed upon me several times that morning not to go into town with Owen. I was about to tell Owen that I would not be going with him, in obedience to God, but when I went to tell him, the thrill of being with him suddenly seemed more important. I ignored the Holy Spirit and went with him anyway. Big Mistake!

Sadly, it was a day full of sin. Owen was in the "get it done work mode" and I was in a "romantic sort of day with my husband mode," and never the twain shall meet.

When we take the truck to town we put all our supplies in the bed of the truck and go from one store to the next, making it risky to leave the truck unattended. When Owen is in the mood and there are not many bags full of purchased items in the back, he'll move the bags up into the cab so we can lock the truck and go shopping together.

We were in the Walmart parking lot with only three bags to move up into the cab in order for us to go into the store together. Owen didn't want to move the bags into the cab of the truck and expected me to go in shopping alone. Of course, I wanted us to go in the store together and he wanted me to just get it done.

My mind went into, "If he loved me like he did in the beginning months of our relationship those bags would have been moved without hesitation! Does he or does he not love me? Obviously not like he once did." I don't know if I'm the only woman who thinks like this, but it's very disturbing and it's not easy being a woman. I interpret all of Owen's behavior and actions with a thermometer of love. He on the other hand carries out his actions based on practicality. Men and women don't always think alike. Men are basically not as sweet and emotional as women. Not to say that's a bad thing, it's just something the Lord uses to help us grow in patience, love and understanding. I doubt if he equated not moving the bags to how much he loved me, but I did that day.

I calmly told him, "Move those bags into the cab of the truck so that we can go into the store together." He said, "No, I don't want to move them." I insisted that he should and he barked back at me and said, "So who's the man of the house, you or me? You want to be the boss?" I told him as I was getting out of the car, "I'll go in the store alone, but you'll regret your decision!" Off I stormed. In my thinking, when a woman goes into the store under those conditions the sky is the limit as far as any budget is concerned.

In the meantime Owen was feeling frustrated with me. The Lord was working on his heart to bring him to a calm forgiveness. I wasn't quite to the door of Walmart when Owen decided to put the bags in the cab of the truck and come and go shopping with me. By the time he got to the store I'd disappeared into the maze of shoppers. It was a Friday before a holiday and the store was packed. Owen was attempting to locate me, his neck got plenty of exercise that day with his head bopping back and forth looking up one isle and down another trying to find me.

I was hurt and feeling dejected while I was trying to find the items on the list. On this particular day one of the items on my list was needles for my sewing machine and they were not easy to find. Because I was still mad I started buying things I would not normally buy, things I'd wanted to buy in the past but didn't due to our budget.

Owen finally found me and said "I was wrong, I'm sorry. Please forgive me." I asked him, "What are you doing here?" He replied, "It's a free country!" I proceeded to wad up the list into a crumpled paper ball and threw it on the floor in a blast of temper, the language that came out of my mouth was anything but pure and holy. I told him, "If you are going to stay in the store give me the keys to the truck and I'll wait out there. I don't want to be anywhere near you." Owen walked away and I continued to fume, feeling unloved and unwanted. Not to mention the heavy ugliness I felt for all the sin I had just committed. Unknown to me, Owen secretly kept an eye on me he later told me.

Well, Owen met me at the checkout stand. By then I had been able to calm down a little, however the dispute put a damper on the rest of the day. The joy of the Lord had seeped out of our day due to the disobedience that we had committed.

Now I was wishing I had obeyed the Holy Spirit when He told me not to come with Owen to town. When we don't listen and obey the Holy Spirit it does not work out well for us. My initial intention was love for my husband. I didn't want to hurt my husband and have him think I did not want to be with him so I went even though the Holy Spirit had told me not to. I made an idol out of Owen by making Owen more important than God's will. It was wrong.

I had to confess my sins; there were so many that it took me the whole day to figure it all out. During the dispute I despised and disrespected Owen. I disobeyed the Holy Spirit. I used foul language and became angry. My anger took root in unfulfilled expectations. I expected him to want to go into the store with me as much as I wanted to go into the store with him. Most importantly I grieved the Holy Spirit.

The Bible says in 1 John 1: 9, "If we confess our sins, He is faithful and just and will forgive us our sins and cleanse us from all unrighteousness."

I confessed all my sins to God and asked God to forgive me, and I also asked Owen to forgive me. Now that forgiveness was done, still the guilt of my sin weighed on my shoulders for a long time. Of course, Satan, the great accuser, loves that.

I needed to cry out, "Help Me God." God told me to confess my sin, which I did. It's up to me to believe God when He says He will forgive me and cleanse me from all unrighteousness. I have to ask God to increase my faith when I'm condemning and shaming myself for something I've already confessed to God. God did not want me to live in guilt and condemnation. God wanted me to trust Him. He heals us in His own way and in His timing.

Owen was often times at his wits end because my emotional needs were beyond his sense of normalcy. The Lord spoke to Owen during a quiet time after our Bible study one morning and told him, "Drink your C.U.P.!" He asked, "What is my C.U.P. Lord?" God told him, "**Compassion, Understanding and Patience**." C.U.P.

We all have to drink the C.U.P. when it comes to living at peace with others. We will face agitations, frustrations and misunderstandings when dealing with people and when accepting our own short comings. Drinking the C.U.P. is not easy, but all things are possible with God. This C.U.P. equates to love and that's what God wants from us, love. Owen said the Holy Spirit impressed upon him that the "C" of compassion had to always precede the "U" of understanding. The "C" of compassion enabled him to remain calm and quiet so that he would not just think of himself but he could think of how I saw and felt about a situation. This took compassion. By being able to keep his mind relaxed he was able to understand my needs. Once the "U" of understanding was established he could then move on to the "P" of patience. Patience allowed him to NOT do what comes naturally by reacting in anger. Now, drinking from the C.U.P. of compassion, understanding and patience allows him to respond lovingly with mercy and grace.

Two commandments in the New Testament sum up the Ten Commandments of the Old Testament: it says we are to "Love the Lord your God with all your heart, mind, body, soul and strength," and "Love your neighbor as you love yourself," as stated in Luke 10; 27. First the love of God must enter us and then we can genuinely feel love for others. This certainly includes our spouses. C. U. P. can be used with anyone we find challenging to love. Compassion, Understanding and Patience can carry us over a lot of rough roads. Owen is further along than I am, but I trust and know that God is moving me in the right direction too.

Loving people is not always easy. We battle with our selfish nature and we annoy, agitate and anger others. We long for others to have compassion, understanding and patience with us. When we are the recipients of an attack, it's an opportunity for us to please the Lord, not ourselves. The challenge is being compassionate, understanding and patient with them. It's our chance to love in this way. It's a hard choice when we're in the midst of being challenged with someone, but we can have victory through the power of the Holy Spirit at work within us. We should pause during that critical time before we are about to react and ask God to help us right there on the spot to think about this C.U.P. lesson. If we fail, we must remember to ask

God to forgive us and keep asking for His help to become more successful. It will get better.

Helpful Ideas

Scriptures to read and consider:

♥ **Proverbs 15: 1-2 (NIV)**
A gentle answer turns away wrath, but a harsh word stirs up anger. The tongue of the wise commends knowledge, but the mouth of the fool gushes folly.

♥ **Matthew 5: 5 (NKJV)**
Blessed are the meek, for they shall inherit the earth.

Read the following scriptures, then choose one and meditate on it:

♥ **2nd Corinthians 12:9 (NIV)**
But He [God] said to me, "My grace is sufficient for you, for My power is made perfect in weakness."

♥ **1 John 1:8-9 (NKJV)**
If we say that we have no sin, we deceive ourselves, and the truth is not in us. If we confess our sins, He is faithful and just to forgive us our sins and to cleanse us from all unrighteousness.

♥ **Ephesians 3: 16 (NASB)**
That He would grant you, according to the riches of His glory, to be strengthened with power through His Spirit in the inner man.

♥ Never forget that God loves you and always will. There's nothing that you have done or ever will do that is able to keep God's love and forgiveness from you once you have accepted the Lord Jesus Christ as your Savior. Confess your sins as they come up and ask God for forgiveness. Trust the Holy Spirit to be the power you need to help you.

♥ Pray for the people that you have hurt through your sinning and ask them to forgive you. That's not always possible, but if that opportunity is available to you, it's the best choice. Sometimes your sins have hurt people so badly that they are not capable of forgiving. Pray for them to forgive you for their sake. Forgiving others is not a request from God; it's a necessity as stated in the Bible in Matthew 6:12 – *"And forgive us our sins, as we forgive those who sin against us."* The more egregious our sin toward others the more prayer needed on their behalf. If you've killed someone, the family of that person is going to need lots of prayer to get to the point where they are able to forgive you and you may never know they have forgiven you.

♥ Sadly, at times we make terrible choices that affect others negatively and it can change lives forever. Repent and ask God to forgive you. Believe that Jesus died on the cross for you, because He did. He loves you despite the way you feel about yourself and He always will. If you want to please Him, then trust and obey Him. Read His word and find out what He's all about. Start with the book of John in the Bible, then move to the book of Ephesians, also located in the New Testament.

♥ Eventually, as a new believer you'll read through the New Testament, Proverbs and Psalms. As time goes on and you grow in your faith, the Old Testament will become more and more interesting.

♥ Sin is sin, whether it's gossiping, jealousy, pride, murder, hate, envy, lying, taking the Lord's name in vain, etc. When you sin, quickly repent and ask God to forgive you and don't worry, but believe your sins are forgiven in Christ Jesus.

River Rock Talk

Owen and I are kindred souls, we both love the outdoors. Not in any kind of stressful way like a three-mile jog or anything that would make us sweat, but rather in the surrounding beauty of a leisure hike and if I have my way, it would be more of a stroll.

We live on the bank of a river in southern Oregon. The southern coastal part of Oregon is spectacular. Bathed in the beauty of God's creation with big green fir trees, moss covered boulders, ferns, wild roses, tiny green tree frogs that can be seen hidden in the petals of a rose, and beautiful rivers that flow into the frothy ocean.

Owen and I were on the river bank looking for unique rocks. Since we moved here we find rocks that sparkle in the sunshine. I confess that it is more me than Owen that looks for the sparkling beauties. Owen keeps an eye out for rocks that he can use in building projects like stone walls, walkways and landscaping.

We were walking along the shore of the river when Owen found a particular rock that he thought would be beautiful if broken open. He was trying to impress me by throwing down the rock onto another bigger rock to break it open and show me the beauty that was hidden within. That's when the Holy Spirit quietly spoke to Owen and told him, "Don't throw that rock." Owen paused for a few seconds but didn't obey and threw the rock onto another larger rock right in front of where he was standing. He threw it hard and it broke into pieces. A chunk went flying into his leg, cutting his shin and bruising him. It was bloody. Owen yelled out, "Dang, I knew I shouldn't have done that!!"

The Holy Spirit talking to Owen taught him a lesson. When we don't obey the Holy Spirit it can have brutal and possibly deadly consequences. Sadly, the rock that Owen broke wasn't any different inside than it was outside.

In John 10:27, Jesus said, *"My sheep recognize my voice. I know them, and they follow me."* Jesus specifically lets us know that we will recognize God's voice when He communicates with us.

Psalm 46:10 says, *"Be still and know that I am God."* When a parent tells a child to "Be still," we know that declares, "Stop what you're doing and be calm." That statement also indicates control and authority. The wonderful thing about our situation is that God loves us just as we are. He sees and knows all and wants to help us. Stop what you're doing and relax. Be still and listen. He's watching and may want to speak to your mind.

Helpful Ideas

♥ Read Romans chapter 8 and 2nd Corinthians chapter 5.

♥ Think about this: The Holy Spirit is God. He's God with us and living in us but only if we are saved. I realize this is an unbelievable concept to some; however, it's the truth. The sooner we accept this truth the sooner help for our daily life will be made available through the power of the Holy Spirit. The Bible is the true Word of God and God uses it to speak to His children all the time. Reading the Word of God is of utmost importance. Pray a little prayer before reading the Bible and ask for God's help in understanding what is being said in scripture. It's always good to also let God know that you want to get to know Him better for a closer relationship with Him.

♥ Talk to God. He's longing to hear from us. The Holy Spirit chooses many ways to communicate with us.

♥ It is important to be very clear right from the beginning of what the Holy Spirit will and won't do in your life here on earth. The Holy Spirit will not indwell you apart from being saved. Once you are indwelt by Him, consider what He does and does not do.

The Holy Spirit **won't** do the following;

♥ Will not tempt you to sin or cause you to do anything evil or wicked.

♥ Will not lie to you.

♥ Will not condemn you.

♥ Will not go against the teachings and truth of the Bible.

The Holy Spirit **can and will** do the following;

♥ Will counsel you.

♥ Will help you.

♥ Will comfort you.

♥ Will lead you into all truth.

♥ Will convict you of sin and evil.

♥ Will help remind you of all the teachings of Jesus in the Bible.

♥ Will be the power you need to battle evil and sin in your life.

♥ Will be with you always, here on earth and into eternity.

Now when Satan whispers in a saved person's ear that they are not forgiven, it's a lie. Jesus died on the cross and said, "It is finished." His death covered your sins of yesterday, today and tomorrow. We will occasionally sin and what is even worse is intentional sin which is something we should avoid at all costs. We do need to confess our sin and ask forgiveness with a sincere heart. You may repeat the same sin over and over again and need to confess the same sin many times before finally your bad behavior changes.

Trust God to use the power of the Holy Spirit to strengthen you to make better choices that will lead you away from sin and into holiness. He'll do it. He'll help you. Keep asking for His help. He is known as the "Helper." The Holy Spirit will continue to be the power you need to live this Christian life following closely after Jesus' teachings. Don't be hard on yourself, rather come to the Father and let Him know that you can't do this alone and you need Him. The Father sent His Holy spirit to be there for you. He loves you despite your inability to be perfect. He's perfect for you. He does expect you to do your best to obey Him and come to holiness and Godly maturity.

Mansion

Owen and I were in the midst of having our prayer time when a disturbance broke out. Looking back now it almost seems humorous, but at the time it led to a volcanic eruption.

During our morning prayer time we were thanking God for the mansions He's prepared for us in heaven like the Bible says in **John 14:2-3 (NKJV),**

> "In my Father's house are many mansions; if it were not so, I would have told you. I go to prepare a place for you. And if I go and prepare a place for you, I will come again, and receive you unto Myself; that where I am, there ye may be also."

The hot lava within me started to bubble up when I heard my husband thank God for his mansion and how he hoped that it would be next to mine. Next to mine, I thought. Doesn't he know we live together? I was hurt and the volcano exploded. Did he not want to live with me in heaven? Right away I started to speculate who he was going to invite to his mansion that would make it necessary to exclude me. Why did he want to shut me out of his life? I did not want to be without him for a moment and here he was thanking God for a separate mansion. Well, needless to say our prayer time came to a screeching halt.

Naturally we had to talk this out for about an hour. It was a very loud conversation. Owen told me, "I really want one mansion for both of us, but I don't know if that is possible." Of course me being the "know it all" knew what was and was not available in Heaven. Too funny. I just want to say right now that God must get a kick out of us. We're funny sometimes in a needy pitiful sort of way. It was then that Jesus told me, "Am I not enough for you? When you get to heaven it won't matter if he shares his mansion with you. I love you."

After these words from Jesus I at once felt humbled, corrected and loved. The other thought that occurred to me was how easy it was to make another human an idol. In my heart at that moment Owen was more important than God and ultimately I was more important than either one of them. I at once apologized to God and Owen, they forgave me and we had to start-over.

Owen and I do "start-overs" periodically. The rule of the start over is that everything has to go back to how it was prior to the disagreement with no hurt feelings, as if it never occurred. It's a great tool for a married couple. But start-overs only work when the offended person is willing to forgive. The practice of forgiving is a Biblical principle that will reap benefits for a lifetime here on earth and into eternity.

God always expects us to forgive. It is mandatory. We always need God's forgiveness. Forgive each other first then the start-over can begin. Clearly I was troubled when I heard Owen say he wanted his mansion next to mine. I did not have a peaceful mind at that point. When Jesus spoke to me, He gave me His peace as is promised in the word of God. **2nd Thessalonian 3:16**, says "Now may the Lord of peace Himself give you His peace at all times and in every situation."

Helpful Ideas

♥ The point of this chapter was to reiterate how much God loves us despite the fact that we are very imperfect. On occasion my peace can be temporarily interrupted by disappointments that happen. When the interruption comes I seek God's word and wisdom and pray for overcoming. This always leads me back to His true peace.

♥ **John 14: 27 (NIV)**
   Jesus says, "Peace I leave with you; my peace I give you.
   I do not give to you as the world gives. Do not let your hearts
   be troubled and do not be afraid."

♥ **1st Peter 5: 7 (NIV)**
   Cast all your anxiety on Him because He cares for you.

♥ There cannot be true and lasting peace when our minds are
   filled with lies and confusion that causes chaos and
   disorderly thinking. These negative joy-stealing thoughts
   and actions we choose, or others bring upon us, have
   consequences that can bring on frustration, stress and
   anger. The truth of God's word through Scripture destroys
   confusion, lies and disorderly thinking. With God's wisdom
   our choices become better and so do the outcomes. So the
   truth comes first, then orderly thinking, then peace. This is
   why the Bible says the saved ones have peace that the world
   doesn't understand. Now, this kind of peace leads to joy
   because without lasting peace in our life we can't really have
   lasting joy. So the formula is as simple as this: God's truth
   brings orderly thinking that brings about peace, which
   ultimately brings about joy.

Christ in the Clouds

My husband has his own unique relationship with the Holy Spirit. I'd like to share with you one of his encounters.

Owen was a bachelor for 61 years prior to our marriage in 2012. He shared his home with many people over the years. Many of these people that he shared his home with came to him for help, due to the fact they found themselves in a homeless situation prior to Owen's offer.

Leo was a friend he met in a network marketing meeting. He was a professional tile contractor and asked Owen if he could do some tile work in the backyard in exchange for letting him stay in one of the empty bedrooms for a while. Owen agreed. While working in the backyard doing some tiling Leo ran out of the cement Owen had bought. Leo had some in his truck left over from another job. He told Owen "If you let me have my 50th birthday party here I'll give you my cement and do some extra work on your barbeque and patio." Owen was all for the idea and thought, "Great! Free Cement, free work and a party!" He gave Leo the approval and said, "Let's do it."

Leo worked during the months he stayed at Owen's house. On weekends he worked on the patio and when it was done it was even more beautiful than what Owen had anticipated. The patio and barbeque were done in a colorful Mexican pattern with orange, blue and white tiles. There were tile seats and planters with the same cheerful design all around. All this and an ocean view in the background. There were two upper decks with stairs that led to a Jacuzzi and the top deck had chairs and a comfortable couch for relaxing. I thought it was a James Bond type of bachelor pad and all I could think was, he sure took his bachelorhood seriously.

Leo had come through with his part of the bargain and the party was on. Leo planned, decorated and prepared for the occasion. Invitations were sent out and it was a grand success for Leo. Owen became leery, the guests were "new age" people with strange attire, snake handling, earth worshiping and strange dancing. These guests worshiped nature, the earth, rather than our Creator, which is typical for new agers.

Owen thought that the guests attending Leo's party may have a bad attitude toward Jesus to the point of possibly damaging the expensive acrylic statue of Jesus titled "Christ in the Clouds" created by Thomas Wise. He was compelled to move the statue to his bedroom but didn't. He knows now that this thought was advice by the Holy Spirit to put the statue away from the party. Owen ignored the warning.

He didn't feel comfortable at the party so he went to bed early. The next morning while he was waking up all groggy as usual, he heard clearly a calm voice in his head saying "they broke fingers off the statue of "Christ in the Clouds." He jumped up quickly to verify what he just heard and sure enough two fingers had indeed been broken off. This caused Jesus to have a hand sign that presumably meant something to the guests. Fortunately the two fingers that had been broken off were laying on the table below the statue. Owen super glued the fingers back on the hand, but "Christ in the Clouds" was flawed and was never the same. Owen enjoys the Jesus statue but he knows that it is nothing to be worshiped; he owns it because it reminds him of Jesus, and Owen's love for Him.

When the Holy Spirit speaks we must be willing to listen and obey. He spoke to Owen a warning that putting the statue away would be wise. Owen chose to ignore that warning and was hurt by the consequences of a marred piece of artwork.

Helpful Ideas

Read the Bible scriptures below and meditate on them.

♥ **John 16:13 (ESV)**
When the Spirit of Truth comes, He will guide you into all the truth, for He will not speak on His own authority, but whatever He hears He will speak, and He will declare to you the things that are to come.

Memorize the following scripture.

♥ **John 10:27 (ESV)**
My sheep hear My voice, and I know them, and they follow Me.

Birthday Rescue

Owen had a beautiful day planned for my 62nd birthday to include a town-wide yard sale which was located in a huge park. This is the best yard sale of the year! There's no driving from one sale to the other. If you like yard sales you can imagine my thrill at having all these 100 or so yard sales in one location. Talk about a great birthday gift. Occasionally my mother-in-law, Crystal, sends me $100.00 for my birthday so the money for the yard sale was not going to squeeze our family budget.

A couple of months prior to this, Owen had purchased the MacGyver series, only it was incomplete. After we say our prayers at night Owen and I watch peaceful programs to ease ourselves off into a blissful sleep. For instance, we have many series including: Leave It to Beaver, Father Knows Best, Donna Reid, Andy Griffith, Ozzie and Harriet, Little House on the Prairie, Highway to Heaven, The Bob Newhart Show, and other shows.

Owen had been talking to me about the MacGyver series. We found it the month before at a different yard sale and we bought it even though it was not complete. Now at this yard sale we found some MacGyver DVDs that were also not complete. The man wanted $10.00 for all three or $7.00 for two. We weren't sure these were the DVDs we needed to complete our series, but I was fairly sure on two of them. Owen thought we should buy all three, which we did, and when we arrived home we couldn't wait to compare. They were the exact DVDs that were missing in order to make our own MacGyver series complete.

We were both grateful to God for this find as we'd tried to purchase them on the internet and they were too expensive for our budget. This may seem insignificant and trivial to some but we know God is interested in every aspect of our life.

We left the yard sale a bit early to attend a memorial service. The thing about a memorial service is that it can be either a depressing event or a celebration. The two outcomes are based on choices the person being memorialized made while on this earth. In this particular memorial it was a celebration. Because this man, Mark, had become a Christian and therefore, has now gone home to heaven to be with the Lord.

We decided to go out to dinner after the memorial service, Owen asked me, "Where do you want to go for dinner?" Normally I prefer Chinese food, but Owen had recently taken me to a very nice place where the Pastor's wife had recommended their famous ribs. So I mentioned several places to Owen and he was in favor of the ribs.

Unfortunately to get to that restaurant was a struggle due to a closed bridge. So we had to take a detour and we came to a stop light at a busy intersection. It was red when we approached and of course we stopped. Suddenly, Owen had an extreme sense of danger come over him as soon as the light turned green and immediately the Holy Spirit caused Owen to blurt out "LOOK BOTH WAYS!" This was out of the ordinary for him; he rarely panics. After he said that, we proceeded a few feet into the intersection when he slammed on the brakes.

An SUV went speeding through the red light about 45 miles per hour. We are thoroughly convinced that the Holy Spirit saved us from a tragic accident. All of this happened within a split second. When I heard Owen say out loud "LOOK BOTH WAYS" he was not speaking to me; he was speaking out loud as he had been instructed by the Holy Spirit. That SUV would have crashed into the side of the van where Owen was sitting. We both would have been injured badly, if not killed.

As the SUV passed I believe I saw the driver on the cell phone, probably not even aware of what she had done. Thank God for God's divine guidance. Just after the incident we were in tears of gratitude for what God had done for us. We thought right then we either could be dead or suffering tragically in a hospital and our lives would have been changed from that point on. The Holy Spirit is alive and well and wants to communicate with us, protect us, heal us, and help us in many different ways.

At the end of my wonderful birthday while we were lying in bed saying our prayers, we thanked God with tears in our eyes again that we were not in the hospital in a world of hurt or even dead. This was not the first time God had saved our lives.

Helpful Ideas

- ♥ Thank God for the last time He came to your rescue.
- ♥ Thank God for the people that love you.
- ♥ Thank God that He loves you.
- ♥ Thank God that Jesus was willing to die for you.
- ♥ Think about being more grateful this week.
- ♥ Think about being kind to someone you don't want to be kind to.
- ♥ Think about what it would be like to be that person. Ask God to give you understanding for that person and then pray for that person.

Vanity and Pride

Owen and I belong to a country church located in a small mountain town in Oregon where God's majestic creation is splashed all over with lush green mountains, a clear gentle river, wild ferns, mossy green tree trunks and shimmering waterfalls.

Each year our Pastor and his wife organize a Valentine's dinner. This year it was going to be held at a Mexican restaurant. The Pastor's wife always makes it special by giving every attendee a creative keepsake as a reminder of the occasion. My favorites are the keepsakes she personally makes by hand. This year it was a lovely red heart decorated and painted on a piece of wood with the year inscribed.

While preparing for the celebration, I was praying to God and asking Him to help me find something impressive to wear that would help me look and feel beautiful. The Holy Spirit spoke and told me, "Clothe yourself with the Cloak of Humility." Ouch! One of the most important characteristics of a Christian is humility and not vanity. For the Holy Spirit to tell me to clothe myself with the Cloak of Humility was an indication that I may have a pride problem. That's concerning. Oddly the next thought that came to my mind was humor. For some reason it hit my tickle bone and I started giggling.

The best way to describe how I hear the Holy Spirit is like an audible voice into my consciousness. I've asked the Holy Spirit to help me find something to wear many times before and He's always helped in a practical way by guiding me to an outfit that I would never have put together on my own. In other words, mixing and matching different items and ending up with a fantastic outfit. So this time when He told me verbally from His Spirit to my spirit to put on the Cloak of Humility, I was surprised and humbled.

Helpful Ideas

♥ The opposite of humility is pride. The Bible says pride comes before a fall. When the Holy Spirit told me to put on the Cloak of Humility, He was helping me to fight my pride. Pride has the potential to destroy an evening.

♥ We as women like to look pretty; I think that God made us that way. There's nothing wrong with wanting to look nice, the problem lies with pride. Do we have to think we look better than anyone else? Do we think our worth comes from how we look rather than who we are? Sadly, I don't think there's been a time in history or a society that has existed like that which exits today, emphasizing our outer beauty and body image in such a blatant way, equating a woman's beauty to her self-worth. It's a lie and yet many find themselves trapped in that mind set. We are bombarded with commercialization on a consistent basis, promoting women's pride, especially associating it with how we look. It's no wonder the Holy Spirit was telling me to put on the Cloak of Humility. It actually breaks my heart knowing all the people, young and old alike, who don't feel good about themselves because they don't live up to the images that are portrayed by the mass media.

♥ **The Bible tells us in Colossians 3:12 (NIV)**
Therefore, as Gods chosen people, holy and dearly loved, clothe yourselves with compassion, kindness, humility, gentleness and patience.

Imagine, if we did that how joy filled we'd be! Pride has the potential of touching every aspect of our lives and it leads to dissatisfaction. For instance, if you apply for a promotion and don't get it and you know the person who was promoted, pride can rob you of the joy you may have otherwise shared with the person who was promoted.

Perhaps you're the person who did get the promotion and if so, the best thing to do is to think about how to be gracious to the other applicants and fight the pride that could start to take root in your heart.

♥ There are always going to be people who are prettier, handsomer, smarter, more talented, funnier, more popular, wealthier, stronger etc. … and we have to let go of the pride that will cause us to envy, covet and end up disliking them and cling to humility so that we will allow ourselves the blessing of being kind to them. When I find myself giving birth to the root of resentment, jealousy, anger and other negative thoughts toward another and tension rises, I try to remember to pray for that person and I don't stop praying until my attitude toward them changes - and it does.

Every time I think of them I'll send out a prayer for their blessing. At times my prayer list is long! I try to focus my prayers for people in a practical way. For instance, the person who received the promotion, I'll pray for their success and if an opportunity to help them arises that's an added blessing. Keep on praying for them until you begin to feel kindness for them.

♥ Just think of how many lives are ruined because of pride. Many people who struggle with pride also struggle with greed and envy. Do we need all the things that forces us to work a 60-hour week with no time left for our families? There is nothing wrong with having nice things if God gives us the provisions to afford them, however, the Bible says to:

Keep your lives free from the love of money and be content with what you have. Hebrews 13:5 (NIV)

♥ Another thing we do to conjure up pride is start comparing ourselves to others. We can fight that thought process with the word of God as the Message Bible says in **Galatians 6:4 (MSG):**

Make a careful exploration of who you are and the work you have been given, and then sink yourself into that. Don't be impressed with yourself. Don't compare yourself with others. Each of you must take responsibility for doing the creative best you can with your own life.

♥ If you trust that the word of God is true, and it is, then take to heart what God says and do not compare yourself to others. You will be so pleased with the amount of stress this alleviates from your life. When you submit your ways of thinking to how God wants you to think, God will reward you. The Bible in **James 4:6 (NLT)** says:

God opposes the proud but shows favor to the humble.

♥ Which one of us would not want the favor of God?

The following Bible scriptures will help to focus and reset your mind on correct thinking regarding humility and pride:

♥ **James 4:10 (ESV)**
Humble yourselves before the Lord, and He will lift you up.

♥ **Jeremiah 9:23 (NIV)**
Let not the wise boast of their wisdom or the strong boast of their strength or the rich boast of their riches

♥ **Philippians 2:3 (NIV)**
Do nothing out of selfish ambition or vain conceit. Rather, in humility value others above yourselves

♥ **Proverbs 8:13 (NIV)**
To fear the Lord is to hate evil; I hate pride and arrogance, evil behavior and perverse speech

♥ **Proverbs 11:2 (NIV)**

When pride comes, then comes disgrace, but with humility comes wisdom.

♥ **Proverbs 13:10 (NIV)**
Where there is strife, there is pride, but wisdom is found in those who take advice.

♥ **Proverbs 16:5 (NIV)**
The Lord detests all the proud of heart. Be sure of this; they will not go unpunished.

♥ **Proverbs 16:18 (NIV)**
Pride goes before destruction, a haughty spirit before a fall.

♥ **Proverbs 16:19 (NIV)**
Better to be lowly in spirit along with the oppressed than to share plunder with the proud.

Benefits of a Christian Life

Nothing could be richer or more rewarding than the truly devoted Christian life of faith. We who are saved in Christ have wonderful spiritual blessings. Consider the following blessings for the true Christian:

♥ We have complete forgiveness available to us once we confess and repent of our sins.

♥ We have an inheritance beyond anything we could imagine awaiting us in Heaven.

♥ We are privileged children of a perfect, loving and holy eternal Father. He is perfectly wise and gives daily blessings.

♥ We have complete security of our eternal future.

♥ We are alive with new life here on earth.

♥ We are God's masterpiece.

♥ We are in union with Christ.

♥ We are members of one large and growing body of believers who are our spiritual brothers and sisters and where ever we go we can find them.

♥ We have access to God the Father thru Jesus Christ our Savior who promised us the gift of the Holy Spirit who indwells us. And therefore, we experience power having God with us and working through us in our life.

♥ God hears our prayers.

♥ We have purpose.

♥ God blesses us with favor and protection and all the wonderful promises written in the Bible that are for His children.

What extraordinary statements. How great is the Christian life when seen in the light of our salvation in Christ. Moreover, we do not have to earn this exalted position. All this and more is already ours through our salvation in the Lord Jesus. Why would anyone not become saved and have these benefits to help their current life now and into eternity?

Consider This

The reason this chapter is being presented to you is so that you may think about coming to salvation in Christ and enjoying eternal life in heaven. Jesus is reaching out to you.

A.W. Tozer says this:

> *"God's justice stands forever against the sinner in utter severity. The unclear and feeble hope that God is too kind to punish the ungodly has become a deadly opiate for the consciences of millions. It hushes their fears and allows them to practice all pleasurable forms of sin while death draws everyday nearer. And the command to repent from sin goes disregarded. As responsible moral beings we dare not trifle with our eternal future."* [2]

Jesus came from heaven to bring people to the truth and to be the only perfect payment for a person's huge sin debt. Turn away from your sinning and put your faith in Jesus and obey His teachings. Make Jesus your Lord and Master so you may be saved from God's perfect and holy judgment of your sin life. You must do this before you die; afterward is too late. Please know that God's holy and perfect judgment will happen following the day you pass from this earthly life.

Attend a God loving and Bible centered church this Sunday and please surrender your life to the Lord Jesus.

---

[2] A.W. Tozer, "Knowledge of the Holy." Moody Publishers/Harper Collins Publishers, 1961.

Salvation Prayer

(Similar to a prayer found in a book called, "One Thing You Can't Do in Heaven," by Mark Cahill)

Dear God,

I have sinned against you by breaking Your Commandments. Despite the conscience of right and wrong that You gave me, I have lied, stolen, I have made up a god in my mind to suit myself, I have looked with lust, and thus committed adultery in my heart. I have been covetous, and harbored hatred in my heart which makes me guilty of murder in Your sight. I've used Your holy name in vain, and have dishonored my parents.

If I stood before You in Your pure holiness on Judgment Day, if every secret sin I have committed and every idle word I have spoken came out as evidence of my crimes against You, I would be utterly guilty, and justly deserve separation from God and to be cast into Hell.

I am unspeakably thankful that Jesus took my place in judgment by suffering and dying on the cross. Jesus paid my fine so that I could leave the courtroom. Such wonderful mercy and grace You have for me. By doing this ultimate sacrifice, You revealed how much You love me, Father.

I believe that Jesus then rose from the dead, according to the Scriptures. I now confess and forsake my sins and yield myself to Jesus to be my Lord and Savior. My sins will now be behind me and I'm not to be judged by them forever more. I will no longer live for myself alone. I present my body, soul, and sprit to God as a living sacrifice, to serve Jesus in the furtherance of His Kingdom.

I will read the Bible daily and obey what I read. When I fail, I will confess my sins in the name of Jesus and ask for your continuing forgiveness and cleansing. I also ask for the Holy Spirit, to come now and live in me, to help me overcome my weaknesses, my failings and any future sinful temptations. It is solely because of Jesus resurrection from the grave that I will live forever in Heaven. I am eternally yours Jesus.

And in Jesus' name I pray. Amen.[3]

---

[3] Similar to a prayer found in the book, "One Thing You Can't Do In Heaven," by Mark Cahill, Biblical Discipleship Publishers/Genesis Publishing Group, copyright 2002/2011.

Holy Living

This is an excerpt from "Cultivating Holiness" by Joel R. Beeke: [4]

Develop a scriptural formula for holy living. Here is one possibility drawn from 1st Corinthians. When hesitant over a course of action, ask yourself:

Does this glorify God? .... *1st Corinthians 10:31*

Is this consistent with the Lordship of Christ? ...... *1st Corinthians 7:23*

Is this consistent with Biblical examples? .... *1st Corinthians 11:3*

Is this lawful and beneficial for me spiritually, mentally & physically? .... *1st Corinthians 6:9-12*

Does this help others positively? .... *1st Corinthians 10:33*

Does this hurt others unnecessarily? .... *1st Corinthians 8:13*

Does this bring me under any enslaving power? ...... *1st Corinthians 6:12*

97   [4] Joel R. Beeke, "Cultivating Holiness," p. 407, Puritan Reformed Spirituality, Grand Rapids, Reformation Heritage Books, 2004.

Made in the USA
Middletown, DE
23 July 2021